This Sporting Life, That Sporting Death

THIS SPORTING LIFE,
THAT SPORTING DEATH

John Kiely

SOUTH BRUNSWICK AND NEW YORK: A. S. BARNES AND COMPANY
LONDON: THOMAS YOSELOFF LTD

A. S. Barnes and Co., Inc.
Cranbury, New Jersey 08512

Thomas Yoseloff Ltd
108 New Bond Street
London W1Y OQX, England

Library of Congress Cataloging in Publication Data

Kiely, John.
    This sporting life, that sporting death.

    1. Sports. I. Title.
GV706.K48   796   77-146760
ISBN 0-498-07782-9

Printed in the United States of America

For Harold Krier
(and all of the others)
who held it on the line——
and then slipped over.

CONTENTS

ACKNOWLEDGMENTS

The author thanks the following for permission to reprint from their copyrighted materials:

Advertising, Copyright © 1970, Joseph Schlitz Brewing Company, used by permission.

Death in the Afternoon by Ernest Hemingway, copyright © 1932 by Charles Scribners & Sons, by permission of the publisher.

McCall's magazine, January 1970, copyright © 1969, the McCall Publishing Company, used by permission of the publisher.

Maynard Parker, *Life* magazine, used by permission of Life.

The Encyclopedia Americana, by permission of the publisher, Grolier, Inc. of New York.

Timber Line by Gene Fowler, copyright © 1933 by Gene Fowler, used by permission of Crown Publishers, Inc.

Seven Pillars of Wisdom by T. E. Lawrence, copyright © 1926, 1935 by Doubleday & Company, Inc., reprinted by permission of the publisher.

Cyrano de Bergerac by Edmond Rostand, Brian Hooker Translation, copyright © 1923 by Holt, Rinehart and Winston, Inc., copyright © 1951 by Doris C. Hooker. Reprinted by permission of Holt, Rinehart and Winston, Inc.

Wind, Sand and Stars by Antoine de Saint-Exupery, by permission of the publishers, Harcourt, Brace, Jovanovich, Inc.

Barnstorming by Martin Caidin, by permission of the publisher, Hawthorn Books, Inc.

The American Heritage History of Flight, copyright © 1962 by American Heritage Publishing Co., Inc., reprinted by permission.

Old Soggy No. 1 by Hart Stilwell and Slats Rodgers, copyright © 1954, Simon & Schuster, Inc., by permission of the publisher.

Rickenbacker by Eddie Rickenbacker, reprinted by permission of the publisher, Prentice-Hall, Inc.

The Myth of Sisyphus and Other Essays by Albert Camus, by permission of the publisher, Alfred A. Knopf, Inc.

You Should Have Been Here an Hour Ago by Phil Edwards and Bob Ottum, by permission of the publishers, Harper & Row, Publishers, Inc.

The Heart of Darkness by Joseph Conrad, by permission of the publishers, J. M. Dent & Sons, Ltd. and the trustees of the Joseph Conrad estate.

The Snows of Kilimanjaro by Ernest Hemingway, reprinted by permission of the publishers, Charles Scribner's & Sons.

My Early Life: A Roving Commission by Winston Churchill, reprinted by permission of the publishers, Charles Scribner's & Sons.

The song lyric "Proud Mary," by J. C. Fogerty (of Creedence Clearwater Revival), copyright © 1968 by Jondura Music, Berkeley, California, by permission of the publisher.

Sometimes a Great Notion by Ken Kesey, copyright © 1963, 1964 by Ken Kesey, reprinted by permission of the publishers, The Viking Press, Inc.

"Notes on Dangerous Game" by Ernest Hemingway from *By-Line: Ernest Hemingway* edited by William White, reprinted by permission of the publishers, Charles Scribner's & Sons.

Here's Death, twitching my ear: "Live," says he, "for I'm coming."—Virgil c. 45 B.C.

You only go around once in life. So grab all the gusto you can.—Schlitz beer advertisement c. 1970 A.D.

INTRODUCTION

All of it is there. The dust lifting up out of the arena in the spring, the horses' hooves hitting hard, the sun burning the skin after a cold winter . . . wheels splashing, churning, crashing through mud and water, spraying the thick black ooze back onto you, the ground soft and sucking as you try to run over it. . . . The airstrip hot with heavy summer sun . . . or summer again, but drizzling and gray as the angry little engines begin to sound like swarms of mad insects about to bite into and devour the track . . . sand spraying and dust thick and choking as you get closer with all about you—even the people—dry and hot and cracking like old leather boots too long left outside . . . in an airplane and watching the light line tight face muscles . . . and more. And there are the smells, too—smells that haunt the head with different memories of the same event: castor oil, carbon, dust, horse manure, hot air, sweat, grease on hands, mustard, gasoline, and mud at the corner of your mouth.

All of these things stick in the edges of the mind and come back occasionally to remind, renew and haunt you as you hunt back through your yesterdays.

A little while ago—though longer than yesterday—people kept Sundays for picnics, men went fishing and hunting, or spit tobacco juice and pitched horseshoes. Now it's nothing to tow a racecar a couple of states and rip around a track

chasing skill, time and some measure of courage. A fellow might leave an office door on Friday evening and a plane's on Saturday afternoon. Men and women are purging their spirits of the sin of safety as they engage risk on its own level. The number of such sportsmen is rising. Sky-diving offers an example. In 1956 there were 250 recorded jumps. A decade later over three-quarter of a million were logged.

Why?

There are as many reasons as there are people who do it. And, anyway, why is a question that exists to be unanswerable.

But, in *Death in the Afternoon*, Hemingway wrote: "We in games, are not fascinated by death, its nearness and its avoidance. We are fascinated by victory and we replace the avoidance of death by the avoidance of defeat. It is a very nice symbolism, but it takes more cojones to be a sportsman when death is a closer party to the game."

The symbolism is wearing thin. Today, faced with a sanitary society where danger and death are treated with disgust as white-coated lab men try to wipe them out, where the truth of emotions once born of action are buried in hollow jobs and under carbon paper lives, the danger sportsmen have found rebellion in a game.

What follows are reports on some such games.

This generation and the next need to get back to the dirt.—Steve McQueen

1
MOTO-CROSS

You drive until you come upon them on some Sunday—always some Sunday. When you see them they are like a camp of vaguely real and mostly imagined army preparing for a battle in the distance of your mind.

The roads you have come, at last, upon are never very good. Mostly they are mud, but they can be dirt, packed hard and very dry, or loose dust that spins like snow from under the wheels of your car. Today they are mud. It seems there are always signs that mark your way. The signs are almost always the same, paper with the words scrawled or printed upon them: Cycle Racing Today.

To talk, quickly, about all cycle racing is a preposterous task. There are as many reasons for racing as there are people who race, and there are types of races for types of people. Some are run in stadiums on pavement, some on dirt, some on semi-tracks, and some across the fields. Some are run by the greasy-haired who seem to belong to some past decade and have been nurtured on the sound of straight country and western songs. Some are raced by gentlemen sportsmen in expensive leathers and gleaming helmets. Some are raced by dust-crusted pros in Levis and jerseys and large leather boots. My type is the Moto-Cross. It's of the sort where you discover the place and see the strange army early encamped on Sunday morning.

Moto-Cross is a souped-up European counterpart of the American scramble. The scramble is run on a semi-improved dirt course, with right and left curves, at least a mile around. The semi-improvements are slight: a certain amount of grading, and track maintenance. The Moto-Cross is run on an unimproved dirt track with right and left curves, not less than a mile and a quarter. And an unimproved dirt course can be pretty damned unimproved.

On one particular Sunday the crowd gathered early. The rain had fallen hard all through Saturday and the sky was vaguely clouded at sunrise on Sunday. Soon the clouds drifted away and the warmth of the sun sucked some of the cold out of the November air. The day was bright and warm the way deep fall days are warm in the Plains States. The race course was on an airstrip and the mud was thick and black and oozed up from under the wheels of cars that parked or tried to park. I put on a pair of green high-topped pacs and walked over to watch the riders trying out the track. The sunlight reflected off pools of standing water and made shadows against the rut marks of the jumps. The ground of the track was loose and slick.

An amateur from Colorado was pulling his bike back to his car. He had been out with some other amateurs and some of the European pros.

"What's it like? As bad as it looks?"

"At least," he said squinting up his face. "I just got out when one of the Europeans went in

front of me and kicked a mudball back. It hit me right in the mouth and I said—that's enough—and came in."

"Not going to race?"

"Nope. They can have this one. I'm just going to watch."

There would be plenty to watch.

When you got tired, if you ever got tired, of watching the riders get the feel of the track under their wheels, you could start watching the spectators. The mechanics, doctors and college kids had started coming in in force. The uniform of the day is jeans of some sort, sweatshirts and jackets. I had on a Pendelton, a sweater and a plaid light cruiser. Almost everybody carries cameras, instamatic, still or movie jobs. One poor chap came with a shiny Nikon and a 200mm lens only to find out he could stand right next to the track. Everybody could. Though this was bigger than the typical Sunday meetings, the movement of specta-

tors wasn't restricted as severely as usual. There is much benefit to seeing a first race this way. You can pick out an exciting spot—say a jump—watch a few, or all, the riders take it, then run across to see how they do slopping through high standing water, then check the horseshoe curve. Perhaps finally you'll locate a spot you particularly like where you can see almost all of the track and keep watch on a couple of difficult areas. The only real trouble is getting too interested. Bikes do run out of the track, on purpose and accidentally, and it's wise to keep detached enough from the action to have presence of your surroundings.

The spectators still come in. They cluster in groups, split up, spot friends from previous meets and gather in groups again to drink beer and eat ham sandwiches (although neither are traditional as ham sandwiches are at horse shows) and talk about bikes or babies.

This is part of the sport. The spectators at this

event, this day, have come to watch the top European and American Moto-Cross pros in action. Amateurs and pros will participate in their own races. On another Sunday many of these watchers would be riding their bikes in strictly amateur events in a different county or a different state. The gathering of the faithful to watch is part of the ritual that makes up this sport. It is as if their meeting and talks were the preliminary bout before the main event.

At noon the track gets empty. The last riders have finished fighting for its feel. Others haven't had the chance. Bike repairs and adjustments have held their time. In the pits some bikes haven't moved far from the white CZ truck. Vlastimil Valek, Czechoslovakia's National Champion, is standing near it. Work on his CZs goes on. He's concerned but seems in a beautiful mood. Speaking in Czech he apologized, through an interpreter, because he didn't speak English well enough and

was apologized to in turn because we didn't know Czech. His eyes are blue and they are sharp like pieces of honed steel are sharp. They seem to look through you and beyond until you notice just how happy they are, how they smile in their own way as if saying in a language that needs no interpreter how pleased is their owner who appreciates that you wish to meet him and are interested in his work. Then he says that when he was a small boy in a town in Czechoslovakia all of the big boys rode motor bikes and he knew that he wanted to ride as well or better than they.

It is pleasant to meet someone whose wish has been granted.

The interpreter, who is some sort of CZ representative and is gray-white–haired and amiable but touched with suspicion like a used car salesman, mentions that motorcycle racing, in various forms, is to the Czechs what baseball is to the Americans. He describes, in a sketch of words, numbers of people entering the stands to watch the graceful riders going through the mechanized ballet of a race. And it is here you wonder how

you've reached just this point in time, standing, off a paddock, talking with a famous champion sportsman about a game that couldn't have been before this century began.

I doubt if such statistics are kept, and even if they were, compiling them would be a job, but all across America each weekend from sometime in March until the weather goes bad for good—which depends on where you are—weekends mean cycle racing. In cities and at the edges of cities, small and large, the racers and their spectators gather. The spectators usually number many fewer than those at some little high school basketball game. But there are so many clubs and so many towns you wonder how many people know and watch and join this sport and if they know how it happened to be.

In some ways the motorcycle is backward. The automobile was used and sold before its racing came. The airplane, too. The motorcycle? In a way it emerged at a race.

Oh sure, when bicycles came of age in the 1880s men fooled around by mounting motors on

them. A German, Gottlieb Daimler, was probably the first to stick an engine on a frame. He did it in 1885, but it was a long way from being a motorcycle. In 1900 though, the strange connection was born. A New Yorker, Oscar Hedstrom, took a gasoline-engined bike to Madison Square Garden to pace the riders in a bicycle race. George M. Hendee was watching that race. The great bike-maker lost interest in winners or losers though, because his eyes were watching the pacer and his mind was racing well ahead of any land-based object. Muttering to himself, he left his seat, and soon struck a deal with Hedstrom—"You design a motor-bicycle, I'll make it and we'll sell it." They did. They called it "Indian" and the bikes they made then are classics now. In Europe such business went on but it was America's baby. In 1907 William Harley and the three Davidsons got into the game. The company is still very much at it, supplying bikes to such unlikely-seeming compadres as traffic cops and Hell's Angels. The names of the makes continued to grow until they were litany long in the days before the Great War. Racing was big business here and in Europe. It became standard sport across the country and was featured at state and county fairs. But then the war did come and after it—well, the tin lizzie changed a lot of lives. A mass-produced automobile, cheap enough for almost anyone, was more luxury than most could afford to pass up. Bike sales dropped and the list became a litany of the dead motorcycle makes. Racing went the way of the manufacturers. By the time Roosevelt picked up the pieces from Hoover the only big bike makers still around were Indian and Harley-Davidson.

Europe didn't have its Henry Ford so near at hand, and motorcycles increased in popularity after the war. That popularity maintained interest in racing until it developed into a complex sport with makers vying for supremacy on the track to assure sales for the street. And it simply continued to grow, interrupted at times, but always hanging on until it has achieved the mantle of a bona-fide sport that you can dress up for and take your kids to.

In America the whole bike business behaved like some plant cut off from good soil. It stagnated and when it grew again it was in a lopsided and twisted way. After the Korean War, Marlon Brando and Lee Marvin roared onto the screen and into the public's imagination in a film that might have easily been forgotten: *The Wild One.* What made it stick was its noncelluloid counterpart which flourished in the complacent 50s. By 1957 part of that counterpart, the Hell's Angels, had become a standard phrase and were a bona-fide, certified public menace in California. The attorney general published what was an interesting and amusing collection of gleaned intelligence about the bike banditos. Even if much was subsequently discounted as false it provided a cloud of unwashed, uniformed delinquents who could shroud the safety of society and make us, in our ignorance, quake from coast to coast with scenes of imagined pillage. The upshot was that America responded by roundly condemning the Hell's Angels and anything associated—even if remotely or imaginedly—with them. And bikes were inseparably so associated.

The American Motorcycle Association joined in the condemnation. It helped a little, but as writer Hunter Thompson pointed out, these so-called solid citizens weren't always that different from the Angels. On occasion it would have taken a scorecard to tell them apart. There were many reasons these people had chosen motorcycles. And the leather and chain image has lingered on. In the very late 1960s you could have read a letter to the editors of *Motor Cycle World.* By the way, a cut-a-way is the sleeveless denim jacket that is part of many biker club uniforms.

The letter was written in the defense of motorcycle clubs and contended that lots of good folk (including the writer) had worn cut-a-ways for years. For example there were the Glory Seekers—a club which sported American flags as emblems and never donned the Swastika. The writer further suggested that the "public" should look around and see all of the good big bikers, and their clubs, on the road.

Then the writer offered some personal comments—first off, that she was married and had three children.

And so, at least, one reader wrote.

And the letter shows a certain type of cycle psychology, but is offered only as evidence that the black Hell's Angels' image is a long time lifting. If it hadn't been for a charming Japanese gentleman it might not have lifted at all.

When his piston ring and propeller plant got bombed out in the war, it marked the beginning of the end for the old life of Soichiro Honda. After the last battle was over, the last bomb dropped, Japan started gearing up for the future and Honda was ahead of the herd. Knowing that motor transportation was almost nil and gas severely rationed, he fitted his parts together until they came out Honda. In five years his sales were seven million dollars. That wasn't enough. As he told Maynard Parker, "I wanted to be Number 1 in the world, not just Japan."

Parker, in *Life,* recounts Honda's problems of breaking through the black-leather curtain concluding, "Yet the Honda's svelte, brightly painted, racy design and its advertising slogan—'you meet the nicest people on a Honda'—soon made it acceptable for everyone from grandmothers to Society's Beautiful People."

Today you have only to turn through the pages of the slickest of summer magazines to spot the motorbike ads and note there's a slogan for every occasion.

Perhaps, though, the pendulum swung as far as it could when, in 1968, Yamaha introduced the "Lady Yamaha"—a bright pink bike with step

through frame, white fringed seat, electric starter and automatic clutch.

The times were rapidly changing.

It was a gay new day for motorcycle salesmen. The great American market was ripped open and ripe. As bikes became first acceptable and, finally, fashionable, interest in racing rose. Those who bought the small bikes moved up to the big ones and off the roads. New models followed, geared for open fields that hunters had to walk before. A mini-bike boom brought cycles down to toy-size as the go-kart had the car. People bought motorcycles in Kansas and Ohio. And, just as when you

find two kids with bicycles on the same block, racing had to begin.

Slowly it pulled itself up with only racers, family and then aficionados. Now races have honest spectators who've just come to watch. In late 1968 New Hampshire drew twenty-five thousand to watch a road race, and the boom had really begun.

Now you can come upon them clustered in groups. Men donning battle gear, others sweating over machines and having the sweat mingle with the grease. Then, at last, you hear the high-tuned and hard sound of Sunday-shattering engines. The signal flag swirls and the contest begins. Men and unsolid machines sway around curves, hugging each other as they leap off the track, cleated tires clawing mud as they come back—bone-banging hard—settling in straight to catch that final flag.

You watch them all go around. An American who races for Montessa is out of his protective leather clothes. Water and mud had made them slick. All are in jeans and jerseys now. Faces are caked with mud, eyes blink through it. None are wearing glasses. Dust goggles don't work. They just get covered with mud and blind. It's hard work hauling a 750cc bike through this course that Valek calls "the worst I've ever seen."

Soon Valek's gotten the feel of the track—so have the rest. None can know it too well; it changes with the laps. The constant pounding of the herd of bikes makes the edges drop off the pits where water stands. It's inordinately slick and the trick, if you can call it a trick, is to rev harder and barrel through. Always going and keep going. Many amateurs in their own races slow before the water. Their bikes, choking, sputtering and smoking, cough out. And muddy, weary riders push them to the side to restart damp engines. All the time the pounding keeps changing the course and some water gets dried out of their clothes as they keep at the game. But it splashes back later in the track until it's the straightaway and the people are standing single file, like a tall picket fence, watching the riders go all out, gunning to pass.

Torsten Hallman, a three-time World 250cc Moto-Cross Champion, was out of action. The week before he had been spilled and some ribs were injured. Joel Robert, a Belgian, was the only remaining man on the Husqvarna team. Valek was out to make it a race just for them. Twisting and turning through the rigors of the course Robert came out ahead.

But such a performance was without the awkwardness of a man racing atop a machine. Their movements were like fine horsemen atop good mounts. They were one, bike and rider, swaying, curving, swinging out, leaping and then lapping other riders on the straight stretches. It was a movement like the waters of a river rushing. Each was always a part of that river, even in eddying around turns that threw them at an unholy angle to the earth, even in rising clear of the track and settling down as particles of water splash back from the rocks to be a part of the river again.

To counterpoint such beauty is the smell of oil and carbon, mud and rubber, and the sound that you never lose even after hours of listening be-cause it refuses to be lost in some less active part of your brain. The mud and water, slapping riders and watchers, keeps the ballet from seeming too idyllic or too real. It all is choreographed to that shattering sound of engines revved and running. And in it is much beauty. There's a beauty of man and machine moving together to make it all happen, giving the sport the flow of a fine steeple-chase but keeping the gear-grinding shock of a Southern stock car classic. Suddenly the sounds have stopped. The river has run its course. The race is over.

Part of this sport can belong to everyone—and part just to those who do it. And after it has ended one of the riders could be speaking for all, when he tells you he feels "good, real good," and "tired, very tired." But there's much more, so he adds: "I always feel I've learned something. Every-time I go out, I feel I've learned something."

And you don't have to ask to know that part of what he's learned is about himself. After all, that's part of what this and the other danger sports are all about.

There was never a horse that couldn't be rode;
There was never a man that couldn't be throwed.

2
RODEO

Down. And the dust pops up. But not far, not close to that cloud-clear sky. Just a few seconds ago the chute door swung left and the unbroken bronc came bucking out. Stripe-vested judges eye those spurs. They've got to dig in just right to get a rider enough points. Eight seconds is all he has to stay up there. But that's a mountain exploding underneath and eight seconds is forever.

The pick-up man moves in but it's no use. The world just stopped—fast—and the rider went spinning off watching all those people in the stands keep right on going. Then it's down. And the dust pops up. But not far, not close to that cloud-clear sky. Then up, slightly slowly, and brushing a little dust off his Levis, he limps that ever-so-long way back.

Those who make it a business know it as a brutal one. Its heroes live lives of semipublicity and semiobscurity. But still they are among the specialized sportsmen bred of our century. They start before they're out of their teens, and had better be nearing the top during their twenties because the fast action, hard knocks and tension of the trade make them old beyond their years. By their early thirties it's time to taper off. Rare is the professional who hasn't retired by forty.

Like so many short lives, though, the professional life of the rodeo sportsman is exciting. Rodeo and what surrounds it is a mixture of circus, carnival, spectacle and sport set against the mem-

ory of the work of that magic time when there really was a West. From the start of the Grand Entry to the last buck of a bull, the rodeo is a pageant and a tribute and a sport.

Now the extra events, the contract acts from trick rope artists and show horse riding to the singing of some celluloid western star, plus the jargon-laden comment of the announcer make it more performance and less sport. Though this gaiety is as phony as some Carnie pitchman's banter, it keeps a tarnished sheen of the fiesta, and the fiesta and the rodeo were often mingled in the past.

As an amateur sport the rodeo can't offer such cardboard gaiety, but it can't offer the skill of top pro contestants either. If you're going to take a good long look at the rodeo, though, you should see an amateur one somewhere along the line. Its less skilled performances teach appreciation of the pros. Many amateur events began after the Second World War. Among the better, now, are the college-connected type that emerge each spring.

But while the amateurs offer an interesting sort of the sport, it's got to belong to the pros. In addition to the physical pains and strains, they know the economic ones. Clifford Peter Westermeier summed it up nicely in his *Man, Beast, Dust* when he wrote that no other pro sport had the participant paying for the opportunity to win and yet risk his life doing it.

A blitzed quarterback knows, as he's slowly getting back to his feet, that his week's paycheck will come. The bucked-off rider has no paycheck. He bets his entrance fee that he can do his job well enough to win a prize. Though it's a strange way to operate a sport, it fits the manner in which it all began and the men who've made it go.

The rodeo comes from the heyday and the pay-day of the cowpoke. The game is made up out of his work. And though most people will tell you it's strictly American, don't believe them. After all most of the American West was imported from Mexico, why not the rodeo?

An Irish adventurer and writer named Reid sent a letter describing a rodeo in Santa Fe in 1847. The participants were vaqueros, Mexican cowhands. Truly fine horsemen and ropers, it's natural they'd make a sport of their skills.

It wasn't until the 1870s and 80s that the sport spread out through the United States. These were the days of the great cattle drives. Texas law proclaimed, in 1871, that cattle driven North of that state's borders required a brand. Then, with the round-up, the branding began in earnest. With it came demand for skill with the lariat. And just as there were men who could plow a straighter furrow, fire a pistol truer, or draw a better poker hand, there were some men who could outrope others. Eventually, though, someone would get sick of hearing about it, and challenge the braggers to prove their worth. Once, the only price on a wild horse was catching and breaking him. And there were men who mastered that, too. Certainly bronc-breaking ability became a point of contention. As the bets went down the rodeo was born. It was a long way, though, from final form.

With a bond of work and brag uniting people across a lot of country it's easy to see why no

one knows where the first western rodeo was. But when a prize was offered and the contests got bigger, more people took notice of them.

The people of Pecos, Texas, took a lot of notice in 1883. The sleepy little town woke up with a bang that was more than Fourth-of-July fireworks. The action had been a long time building. The boys at the Hashknife thought they had a pretty fair roper. So did the men over at the 101. The Mill-Iron and the W hands and other pokes felt just the same. It was plain to see, it had to be settled. With pay in their pockets and whiskey in their hands they came to get a question answered.

Clearing out the courthouse yard, the wranglers staked it off as their corral. There were taunts and cheers when the top-hands rode up. The corral

31

was full of steers. The day was hot. The stakes were high.

Then the cow-pokes let the steers go, one by one, so the men could show their style. Straight down the main street they charged, lariats flailing the air.

In addition to the roping, another source reports, bronc breaking contests were raising dust in an open field near the town.

This is where a lot of people think it really began. They say Pecos was the first rodeo with a prize and no admission. The distinction is academic and made because it's easier to find the first rodeo where a spectator had to buy a ticket. Only a couple of towns claim that honor, but many places consider themselves host of the first prize rodeo. For example, Cheyenne, Wyoming, claims it for July 4, 1872. Winfield, Kansas, says they were first in 1882. In a way, though, it will be nice if we never find out. Then the whole West can seem to have had the first prize event.

There are those who say that Denver, Colorado, is traditionally accepted as the place where paid

spectator rodeo began in 1887. There are others who will tell you it was Prescott, Arizona Territory, and 1888 (on the Fourth day of July). The Prescott event is, at any rate, the oldest continuous rodeo. It claims another first, too. The grand award was a mounted silver medal. It's the first rodeo trophy. Called the Citizens Prize, it went to Juan Leivas. That makes him the first in a long line of trophy winners. He probably would have rather had the cash.

As the days crept closer to the beginning of the next century and the end of the Old West, rodeos sprang up all over. Meanwhile Buffalo Bill and his imitators threw together Wild West Shows to turn past glory into future profit. They infused a sense of pageant, and performance into the rowdy sport of rodeo. It never went away.

There's a story about Cody which has nothing to do with our rodeo business. But I like it. It's from Gene Fowler's *Timber Line*.

Buffalo Bill Cody once took a knotty problem to Tammen. Now the good Colonel was the handsomest fellow of his time, and no amount of hard liquor could

bloat his stalwart figure, crimson his Alexander-the-Great nose, or otherwise rob him of noble charms that stirred alike the hearts of Kickapoo squaws and Mayfair duchesses.

"However, his vasty tippling sometimes affected his target-shooting abilities, and befogged his oratory. His Wild West Show was making him an international character, and his manager, Nate Salisbury, wished to safeguard Cody's popularity."

According to Fowler, the strain grew greater after a performance in Cheyenne, Wyoming. At the time there "flourished" a hatred in Cheyenne for Lead, South Dakota. Well Cody rode McKinley into the arena and shouted out, "Fellow citizens of Dakota . . . I am happy to be in Lead tonight, and away from our recent dreary residence in Cheyenne."

Salisbury caught Cody, when the latter was recovering hard from a drinking bout, and convinced him to sign a contract that said he would drink no more than ten glasses of whiskey a day. If Cody went back on his word he owed Salisbury $5,000. Bill asked Harry Tammen for suggestions as to how he could survive. Tammen, who was soon to be co-founder of the *Denver Post*, was then bartender at the Windsor. He suggested the buffalo hunter spread his drinks out. He said he'd tried. But, getting up at eight, Cody found that by ten he'd always had his limit. Tammen suggested Cody take the whiskey from chaser glasses and Buffalo Bill was soon back in his prime. Salisbury demanded the money, got Bill's answer and took the question to court.

"It is evident," the judge said, "The Colonel is living up to the agreement as worded. True, he shall not drink from a hat, or a tin bucket; but so long as he sips from a chalice made of glass, he may continue, were that glass the size of a water-tower. I rule for the defendant, the plaintiff to pay the cost of this action."

Salisbury never got the Colonel to sign another semi-pledge.

Long after Buffalo Bill's Wild West Show, and the others, folded, the rodeo was still going strong.

By 1916 the rodeo had gone a long way East.

That August one opened at Sheepshead Bay Speedway. It was called the New York Stampede. The next year, Fort Worth hosted the first indoor rodeo at the Stockyards Coliseum, and started the sport on an eleven-month season. Meanwhile that New York Stampede had interested promoters at Madison Square Garden. The war, though, got in their way.

During the 1920s the word rodeo became accepted and was linked, forever after it would seem, to the events it now describes. Until then the name changed according to the place. It was called, variously: stampede, frontier days, stock show, round-up or fiesta, depending upon the location and inventiveness of its promoters. The word rodeo is Spanish. Once it meant cattle market place. This was a public area and—hit by wranglers after round-up—a time for fiesta, and sport. The connection is logical. It was another debt owed the Mexicans who not only supplied the concept of cattle ranching—even using horses to work the stock—but also supplied all of the gear including saddles and the lariat, which in itself is a corruption of the Spanish words la reata—the rope. Now another word, rodeo, had come along to fill a different need. And the word must have seemed just right. In 1926 the Garden offered the first "World Series Rodeo," and promptly declared it an annual event, even though the title's claim was somewhat outlandish. When the new Garden opened in 1929, promoters offered the same event but rebilled it the "World's Championship Rodeo." The sport greatly endeared itself to the promoters. It had topped all similar events in prize money and attendance.

By this time, a new breed had started being born. Now there had been, for the first time, professional rodeo riders and ropers. Leonard Stroud was one, if not the first, of the full time pros. But he wasn't the first to gain fame in a rodeo arena. There's a man the rodeo aficionados speak of like the baseball buffs mention Cy Young. His name was Clay McGonical. He's a legend as a roper.

His first touch of fame came with wild steer roping. It was a big event until it was outlawed in most Western states soon after the 20th Century began. McGonical, and the others like him, turned to calf roping but he hit a landmark in 1919 when he carried off $1,000 from one rodeo for clocking the best time in roping and tying his three calves. There were still other glamorous figures from the past. One was Prairie Lilly Allen, a bright and brave Tennessee girl. She was outstanding in the ladies' bronc riding class and wound up in Hollywood.

There was a different kind of hero, too. This one came from Wyoming where he'd been reared on John C. Coble's ranch. Coble produced a lot of fine rodeo stock, and this hero was a horse. Gene Fowler's description may be one of the most graphic.

Coble was a highly respected ranch owner, and among other things gave to the rodeo chutes the greatest outlaw horse of all time, "Old Steamboat." This ferocious bucker was the wisest, slyest, strongest, most active sunfisher ever seen. He had a roar like that of a lion, and for nearly ten years tossed champion bronc busters from his spine as though they were sacks of oats. Sometimes . . . it seemed as though it were raining cowboys all over the arena.

A younger generation has heard that Old Steamboat was finally ridden by one, Dick Stanley. Yes, but how? It was one of those cloud-bursting days and Steamboat was up to his hocks in mire. That critter was never ridden on *dry ground*. Later he broke a leg while the boys were loading him on a railway car, and had to be shot. It took *three bullets* from a forty-five to polish [him] off. . . .

But Old Steamboat was from another century and the times had changed.

As the sport grew, it lost the carefree charm it had been born with. Tension rose with the prize money and the rodeo entered its dark days.

It was a time when contestants could split prize money with friendly judges and be assured a win. New talent couldn't break through the web of graft. Word of the fixes filtered through. Attendance dropped. The rodeo started to stagnate. There were other problems. Simpler ones. Events were widespread, rules weren't standard and dates weren't arranged on a regional or national plan. Grown up wild, the rodeo needed some pruning now that it had flowered.

In 1929 the gardeners arrived. The rodeo producers formed the Rodeo Association of America. They standardized the point system for bucking and riding events based on the difficulty of the animal and the performance of the rider.

They arranged and reformed other elements,

too. In fact they did about as much as they could. But they didn't represent the rodeo cowpoke and they couldn't speak for him. They could only hope he would follow their lead, but the cowhand is a prime example of the individual in action. The time finally came, though, when even these individualists had to admit to unity in strength. In 1936 they formed the Cowboy Turtle Association.

Nathaniel Green reports that, "According to legend the association's title stems from a remark made by one of the organizers after a long and futile attempt to pick a name. 'Let's take it slow and easy . . . but get to where we started for.' "

They lived up to his suggestion.

Driven together by too-small purses, handicapping rules, false advertising, and other plagues

of the profession, they launched a series of strikes, and treated strikebreakers to a blacklisting. With the top talent gone, most producers and operators soon came around. Prize purses were upped, and the entrance fees were all put into that pot. The rules were altered and forced into conformity. Even some of the false ad claims were dropped. One was the billing of events as a "World's Championship Rodeo." There simply isn't and wasn't such a thing. The champions were picked because of their yearly total of American Rodeo Association points and not because of any one event.

As the tension of the time wore away, rodeoing settled back for a bout of prosperity.

Some things keep changing. Most have stayed essentially the same. The Cowboy's Turtle Association finally renamed themselves the Rodeo Cowboy's Association. They soon established their point system and now name all-round champion and champions in seven separate events each year.

The Rodeo Association of America has changed names a couple of times—to International Rodeo Association in 1946 and International Rodeo Management, Inc., in 1959.

The need for specialized talent, though, has stayed the same. The Rodeo is still a tense sport demanding quick reflexes and lots of skill. But, as has happened elsewhere, this danger sport fell into favor with the amateurs. After World War Two it became a regular and important event among high schools, colleges, saddle clubs and even prisons in this country. We'll look at the college type.

At one in South Dakota it's the only varsity sport. In one Kansas college, some team members have athletic scholarships. In many other schools,

though, its status as a sport isn't even established and it exists in that satellite sphere of clubs and organizations.

But however and wherever it exists, the rodeo now has a place in college and the colleges a place in a growing sports network. Its organization is the National Intercollegiate Rodeo Association. Formed when college rodeo riders representing a dozen schools got together in 1949, it climbed, in two decades, to over one hundred member schools in seven regions offering about fifty rodeos a season. In addition, the organization has established a playoff for the Regional Champions. The purpose of the association is plain. They explain that their goal is to "promote intercollegiate rodeoing on a national scale by bringing national recognition to this activity as an organized and standard collegiate sport" and of course, "to promote interest, understanding, appreciation and vigilance over western life [and], culture."

The obvious effect of such an organization is an increase of amateur contestants and contests. Since the Association doesn't operate under the strict amateur rules of other athletics, cash prizes can be offered. When they are, they're slight and few per event, though. It is a sport played for fun, not money. And as most people, especially the amateur artist, know—when you try to make a hobby a trade the simple fun stops and the hard work begins.

The rodeo has even been exported, unsuccessfully, to South America, Europe and New Zealand, more successfully to Australia and most to Canada where the Calgary, Alberta, event has come to rank with the rodeos of Cheyenne, Pendleton, Salinas (California) and Sidney, Nebraska, as top pro meets.

When you see one of the present big shows it's hard to connect it to those dusty days in Pecos, Texas. It's also hard not to.

All the propaganda tells you this is keeping alive the spirit of the frontier, but Westermeier, who after all is the rodeo historian, didn't find everyone thinking of it so, and he suggests that if the Rodeo cowboys are it is accidental. For them it is the way they make their living—or part of it—for better or for worse it is their business.

There are five main events to the sport: calf

roping, bareback riding, saddleback riding, steer wrestling and bull riding. The most obvious is calf roping. Its lineage is transparent. A direct offshoot of the range-rider's life, the past is reflected in its present. Bare-back and saddle bronc riding are lifted from that work, too. In both, points are based on a combination of the horse's performance and the man's. He must ride eight or ten seconds, spurring away and keeping one hand free. Also with saddle-bronc riding, a rider's feet must stay in the stirrups.

The horses used for these riding events are valuable. A stock contractor is commissioned to supply them. Generally the good bucking horses are halter-broken and somewhat gentle. They explode only when mounted. A flank strap, though, is placed around their hind quarters because any foreign object on the rear of a horse will probably make him jump. When he's bred and reared as a bucking horse to begin with—well.

Mounting is a tricky business. The rider climbs down to rather than up on a bucking horse. An attendant holds the horse's attention—a common way once was by biting hard on its ear. Once on, the rider has to signal that he's ready before the doors swing open and he and horse shoot out. As you probably know, the worst horses aren't the high and showy buckers, but rather the dervishes that stay by the chutes and twirl around. Getting bucked off looks like it would hurt, but even staying on is a constant strain on bones, muscles, tendons and nerves. It's hard to imagine the rider who, at the end of a show, hasn't thought about finding an easier way to make a living.

Calf ropers are usually bulldoggers, too. This event was imported into the arena in 1903. The idea is to race toward a steer, hop down from your horse, catch the steer by the horns and throw it to the ground.

Another addition that's become standard is brahma bull riding. It is the most dangerous event of all. A close look at a mean-eyed Brahma bull is enough to make you wonder how any riders stay on. And, if one doesn't, even after he lands, the hazard isn't over. A horse, even a bucking horse, will try to avoid an object on the ground. A bull won't. When the object is a man the stakes are high. By now you probably know that the rodeo clown is one of the braver sorts of men.

His job is simple—distract the bull until the fallen rider can get out of the arena. As a clown, he can throw away all elements of grace and style. His job is just to keep the rider safe. He can pull the bull's tail, whack him on the side and even toss a tire toward his nose. The clown has become part of the performance.

What about those men who engage in the rodeo today? They come from all across the country. They ply a hazardous trade or they have picked a dangerous hobby.

When you add to the rugged minutes in the arena all of the incidentals of their lives, the professional rodeo cowboy doesn't seem the sort to envy. Since 1941 the rodeo has been a 12-month sport. The rodeo hand has to choose his best possible circuit based on prize money, fellow contestants and distance to travel. He probably covers 30–40,000 miles a year, subjects himself to the worst kinds of weather, and constant changes in climate, shelter and food. If he's roper or bull-dogger he has to transport and quarter his horses as well as himself. As athletes, these men are probably underpaid and overworked.

It's an expensive sport to begin. Old hands size up the young ones quickly and often work out partnerships where the proteges' expenses are paid in exchange for a third to a half of his take. It's especially hard for beginning ropers and bull-doggers. If they don't have suitable horses they must rent them from another roper for, probably, a quarter of what they make. It's an area of economic, as well as physical, danger. And there are no factory teams in the rodeo.

The situation of the amateurs is different from the pros. But the rodeo, even for fun, is a hard and dangerous sport, demanding much skill.

When you stare back at a Brahma bull it's easy to tell he doesn't like you, and you suspect that there are a number of days when he doesn't even like himself. So what's the percentage of risking pain to carry off a prize cup? Especially when the amateur has little chance to last the time out anyway?

If you question these sportsmen, they have answers. But they are like the answers every participant gives. After all, the one who does something is often the last to know why. If not, then he is the first.

T. E. Lawrence was considering something quite different than rodeo riding. It's part of an answer because what he said, while of war, applies to the rodeo riders—and to the other danger sportsmen as well.

"There could be no honour in a sure success, but much might be wrested from a sure defeat."

De Guiche: Windmills, remember, if you fight with them—
Cyrano: My enemies change, then, with every wind?
De Guiche: —May swing round their huge arms and cast you down into the mire.
Cyrano: Or up—among the stars!

3
AEROBATICS

To me it is always the men and the women who matter.

In the end the other things, such as the machines, are only what they do what they do with. And then it is only the men and the women who matter. The machines change—from cloth and wood and wire to metal and glass—but the men and the women remain.

I was in the front half of the cockpit and turned back, watching him.

"Now I'll do a roll. Don't worry, you won't come out of your seat."

I hadn't even been considering coming out of my seat. Now I did, but only instantly, because we were in that roll. I started lifting a camera to my eye. It was an incredibly hard action. I pushed up on it, not believing it could be so difficult and realizing that I was feeling negative g's and all of this was happening in a second or less. But I got the camera up there, and focused a little sharper and was shooting. I was watching, too. And the face of the man behind me was the face of a happy man. It was a man showing another what he could do with a hunk of metal, a motor and an improbable notion—that man could fly. It was Harold Krier. And he is one in that strange breed of adventurous sportsmen who've come to be called aerobats.

The word itself sounds misplaced in time. Slipped out of centuries, perhaps, but serving in an awkward way to signify a graceful game. Watch them—high, wheeling, like gliding birds, moving, playing, and laughing up there beyond the reach of everyman, like Saint Exupery "taking [their] constitutional between Sagittarius and the Great Bear."

And watching these man-made birds move, and swirl, loop and spin away from the world that made them makes them seem less real, less built, less now. It makes them look more like their ancestors, swept out of now and pushed back to then—frail, thin, wonderfully frightened things which were man's one great mechanical expression of man, the one made mechanism that said it all. The one instrument that changed our nature and let us reach out and up and experience the freedom of flight, and the clarity of view from an altitude which makes houses, and certainly the troubles within them, seem too terribly small. If they are like anything of the earth, they are like the night, the desert and the sea—too frightening to be imagined, too wonderful to be real.

Krier was growing up on a Kansas farm. How much closer can one be tied to the ground? "I remember seeing the first DC–2's flying by," he says. "It was a hell of a lot more fascinating than trying to grow crops." Then, in that same quiet voice, "not that there's anything wrong with being a farmer. That's a wonderful thing. But not for me."

But fascination is only that. And as Krier says, "in those days nobody had money." So he joined the army and served as a flight engineer. "After the war I used the GI bill to get a pilot's and mechanic's rating." And so it was started in Harold Krier as it had been started in a lot of others.

It had started in John Moisant. Here was Moisant, at 40, with a near fortune from mining, an acceptable future in architecture, and an urge.

It was 1908 and he was standing outside of Paris with a lot of others—watching. He was watching the Wright brothers put their plane through its limited maneuvers. And that was it. He rushed off to enroll in Bleriot School of Aeronautical Instruction. Deprived of one first, he settled on another, and packed a "passenger" in his tiny airplane then jolted away toward Dover. The first man to carry a passenger across the English Channel.

Back on the continent, he thought it would be great fun to organize a sporting group to tour the United States and offer exhibitions of flying. He found four willing French aeronauts and off they went—in high style, on a private railroad train carrying planes, people, collapsible hangars, portable bunks and fine French wine.

And what a year it was. The country was still raw, then. And the people could delight in these toys. And there was more than just barnstorming. That was a big year for the Belmont air race. And Moisant was there. He arrived with Miss Paris, his striped cat mascot, and proceeded to crash his airplane. He borrowed another and flew after a $10,000 prize in an elapsed time race from Belmont to the Statue of Liberty and back. Although his time seems to have been best, there were a number of charges and counter-charges of rule violations and in the end he was disqualified. So you see, some aspects of flying had already become organized. But judges weren't always sent for. While Moisant's crew performed for some heavy-drinking Texans they learned that their audience wasn't impressed by the performance when revolvers were fired at the all-too-low flying planes.

Then, on the last day of 1910, Moisant crashed and died in a performance for a New Orleans audience.

And that was the end of what the Wright exhibition flight had started in John Moisant.

Flying was as dangerous a profession as it was glamorous. Frank Coffyn commented, "There were five of us who were called the Wright exhibition team. . . . We were under a two-year contract to fly for the Wrights, and I was the only one of the five who completed the contract."

It had started with Eugene Lefebuve, a lively, frolicking man in love with flying. In August of 1909 he went to the Reims air meet and became its court jester by buzzing horses, fields, trees, stands, people and almost anything else that could move or couldn't. He flitted across the sky like a butterfly free at last of its cocoon. In September of that year he smashed his plane into the earth and won the dubious distinction of being the first pilot killed in a crash.

But there were always others to come and fly.

Lincoln Beachey had been waiting a long time. In 1905, a year and a few months after the Wright flight at Kitty Hawk, Beachey wanted an airplane. He had to settle for a balloon. That he could make. And he did, a contemptible looking creature that he called the Rubber Cow. But it took him, like a magic carpet, across the country. And he performed and took up passengers, and patched his Rubber Cow. And, finally, in 1910, the year of Moisant's death, he reached Glenn Curtiss and got an audience.

Beachey was brash and reckless and surly. He couldn't be bothered with assistance or instruction. He climbed in a new Curtiss plane, jerked the stick back, jumped into the air and crashed. Glenn Curtiss was furious. Another pilot quieted him. There was something about this Beachey. He was a man born to fly. So Curtiss, reluctantly, offered another plane. This time, Beachey got in, jerked back on the stick and promptly crashed. But Curtiss kept him on.

A year later Beachey decided to set an altitude record. Curtiss engineers said he couldn't cram enough fuel in his tanks to do any good. But Beachey turned away in contempt. Of course he could do it. And he did. But how? He flew the little pusher almost straight up, up and up until. . . . Until he ran out of gas. Then he glided it back down to a perfect landing. His recording instrument showed 11,600 feet as his top height. Yes. It was certainly a record.

Beachey never bothered the engineers again.

Anyway, he was too busy looking for something else to do. He decided to fly over Niagara Falls. And he did, but so incredibly low—with the spray splattering his airship, the drafts sucking him down, the mist almost hiding his craft from the watchers. And on he went, then skimming the water with his wheels and coursing under, yes under, the bridge.

Then he shifted to San Francisco and started landing and taking off from the roofs of buildings.

Then he raced Barney Oldfield, and hounded Oldfield all around the track, more than buzzing, matching Oldfield's speed and plopping his wheels near Oldfield's head and almost into the seat, then shooting off, at the last moment, to win. Then, in 1913, having a plane modified because Adolphe Pegoud had flown upside-down before he, Lincoln Beachey, had even thought of it and having to do it now, right now, and then doing it and a loop, too. Then through that year doing a thousand or so more loops. And other things.

"My brother wanted speed," said Hillery Beachey, "that's the main thing. And he wanted to be a showman. I remember seeing him make a landing on the back stretch of a race-track where there were trees hanging over the track. He'd level off on one side, then turn under the trees to make his landing. That was somewhere in the Middle West where William Jennings Bryan was talking. I think they both got a thousand dollars a day, Bryan and Lincoln Beachey."

But then it was 1915 and Beachey was being a showman for more than 50,000 people at the San Francisco International Exhibition. And he wanted to thrill what he called "a pack of jackals, eager to be in on the kill." I suppose he did.

From a thousand feet, he dived directly for the Bay, and then they heard it, the ripping sound as the wings came away, and Beachey continued the dive.

Then it struck.

Twenty-eight years old.

Lincoln Beachey is dead.

It wasn't always deadly, though. There was Hubert Latham. He was half English, half French and looked entirely like an Elizabethan adventurer. It seemed as though he was always smoking a cigarette, and his deep eyes betrayed a knowledge which most men do not have. Doctors told him he had tuberculosis and would probably live no more than one year.

Latham was a man with nothing to lose, like the rest of us, but he knew it.

And he acted on it.

When the *London Daily Mail* offered a thousand pounds to the first aviator to fly over the Channel he accepted the challenge as if it were a duel. On his first try, he crashed into the waters, and was reported calmly sitting on his wreckage, smoking a cigarette, when a French destroyer arrived to rescue him. Then Louis Bleriot came into the

game, and it was a duel. The weather was bad, and Latham decided to sleep for a few hours. He left orders to be called. He wasn't. And Bleriot got off before him, to capture the prize.

Still, there were more duels.

When the *Baltimore Sun* offered a cash prize of $5,000 to the first man to fly over the middle of a large metropolis, Latham promptly flew over Baltimore and collected. He went to the big Reims air meet of 1909 intent upon setting some kind of record. He climbed into the sky, then landed, said he'd flown to 1,200 feet and set a fantastic, new altitude record. The judges agreed in part. They acknowledged he'd set a record, but insisted it was 508 feet. He went off chuckling to himself.

Latham was finally killed. And it was the sudden death he'd said he'd prefer. But he was killed by a wounded buffalo while big game hunting in Africa.

There were others, too, in those amazingly imagined years who found adventure in the skies. There were women like Harriet Quimby. Dressed out in a mauve satin flying suit, she was called the Dresden China Aviatrice and became the first woman to cross the English Channel in an airplane. There was Mathilde Moisant, John's sister, who flew exhibitions until her friend Harriet died in an air show crash in 1912.

And, fittingly, it was Richard Harding Davis who put it all into words when he said that flying was the thrill "that makes all other sensations stale. . . ."

It was new and fun and wonderful.

But soon, seemingly too soon, it would all be over.

War would intrude itself upon the world and alter the nature of aviation.

It is fitting that, in this time before the Great War, the term applied to those who flew was birdmen. The word suggests the simplicity of the age, and the art. There would be different words after the war—among them: ace.

Rickenbacker, von Richtohfen, Lufbery, Bishop, Hall, Luke and other names came to claim a different kind of honor and adulation than Latham, Beachey and Moisant, and at the same time innocently paraphrased Field Marshal Douglas Haig's dictum, "Infantry and artillery can win battles—but only Cavalry can make them worth winning."

Rickenbacker wrote: "We were coming together

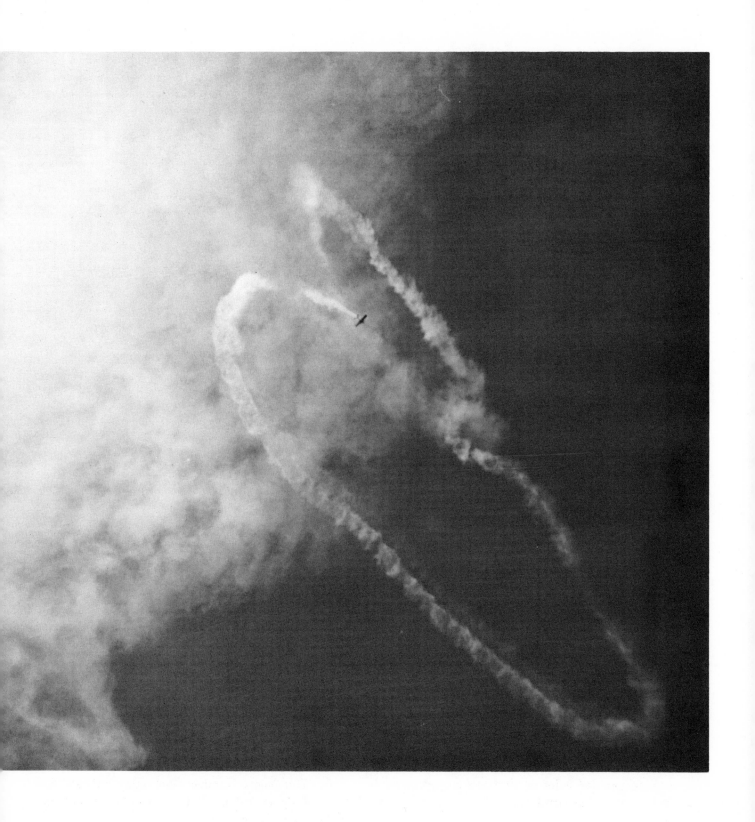

at a combined speed of four miles a minute. I thought that he had better get the hell out of my way. I certainly was not going to get out of his. Just as we were about to crash head on, he dived under my plane. I immediately put my Spad into a renversements—pulled the stick straight back to start a loop and simultaneously rolled it over in a half turn. I came over on his tail right side up and ready to shoot. I gave him a long burst of bullets. He began the long fall down."

For Eddie Rickenbacker, and the others, it was stunting but of a different kind and a different degree. Now a mistake, a wrong move meant more than a loss of form. And those who lived long enough to learn this deadly new trade added their own flying stunts to the airman's repertoire.

The war would end, but not the taste for action and adventure and flying that it started. After that war there were a lot of left over flyers and would-be flyers and a lot of left over airplanes to fly. It was the perfect combination. A little money, a little gas and a lot of guts and a guy could be in business as a barnstormer. And what a business it was.

Dick Depew knows and if you'd ask him what was most dangerous about it he'd probably tell you: "the risk of starving to death."

They were in still a different age, and they knew it. Now there were planes, pilots and interests to move aviation along in different directions— all serious, and all important in its development. Aerobatics, while still an unused term, was one direction. These barnstormers weren't necessarily aerobats though. And what they developed would move in two major directions during this age. While air mail pilots in the early 1920s were getting from $800 to a $1,000 a month, barnstormers were caging coin from small town thrillseekers. At first it was enough to be there. Maybe a couple of low passes over the town then settle into a nice farm field and wait for the locals to come wandering out. "A ride? Sure, an airplane ride? What do you say, mister?" And they charged what they thought they could get, maybe five dollars, maybe a penny a pound. But they were missionaries, whether they knew it or not, and they brought the gospel of air power across a country still marvelling at the Model T Ford.

In "Old Soggy Number One" Hart Stilwell and Slats Rodgers tell of Slats's improbable, but not uncommon, flying career.

"Maybe," he wrote, "we were sort of a mixture of the cowhand of the Old West, the hotrod driver of today, and the real gypsy."

Maybe.

Maybe you were.

Maybe you were, just that.

But soon there were too many in the business and just being there wasn't enough. So they stunted.

"There was a dollar admission fee for the exhibitions," recalls Duke Krantz of the Gates Flying Circus, "but the stunts were just the attraction to get passengers."

Eventually they weren't.

In 1924 the Doug Davis Flying Circus was born. With some fast backing, some shiny planes and some polished acts, they made the flying show a mobile spectacular.

They might have had a corner on the market, but Mable Cody came around. She was beautiful and talented, and she knew what a thrill circus needed. She wing walked, hopped from cars and motorboats to planes and free-fell. She hired a talented crew and a hustling advance man. And it developed into one of the hottest wars in barnstorming history with the Cody and Davis groups at each others' throats. But finally Davis won. Mable's planes fell apart under the strain, and they combined forces and shared the Curtiss candy company's backing to become known by the unbelievable name of "The Doug Davis Baby Ruth Flying Circus." And it was a circus. The stunts were guaranteed to seem even more reckless than they were.

While this was going on, other things were happening in the air. The Schneider Trophy Race continued. It was open to seaplanes of all countries. It was first run in Morocco in 1913. During its history it was run by some of the first craft designed, only, for racing. And it did change the elements of aviation. The Pulitzer Races were for land planes. When they were started in 1920, they were destined to take up where the Gordon Bennett Trophy races had left off. Within two years, the cost of preparation, and racing, was so high all civilian competition had dropped out. It became a race for the military services, and they made the most of it.

In effect the Jacques Schneider race became a military contest, too. It had been established with the intention of retiring the trophy to the country who could grab three wins in a row. The British did in ancestors of the Spitfire fighters of World War II—the Supermariners. Their speeds ranged up to 343 miles per hour.

On other fronts, long distance flights continued. From the 1923 two-day trip across the United States, through Charles Lindbergh's solo flight across the Atlantic, to Wiley Post's 1931 circumnavigation of the world, and his repeat in 1933—this time flying alone.

Aviation was still romantic and nonchalant, but it was acquiring sophistication. The wing-walkers, and daredevil stunt flyers of the 1920s were giving way to a new style—one which might just become an art—aerobatic precision flying. The Navy started a precision team, the Sea Hawks, and others took the tip. Mike Murphy started the LINCO Aces and Tex Rankin and Al Williams brought precision aerobatics to a greater prominence when they performed their stylized stunts before the 1930 National Air Races audience.

But the 1930s belonged to the races and the racers. There was a whole new set of heroes—Jimmy Doolittle, Roscoe Turner, and Frank Hawks, the Meteor Man. There were big races, nationals in Chicago and Cleveland, and new, major trophies, the Thompson Trophy for the fastest speed in a closed circuit course and the Bendix Trophy for transcontinental—the equivalent of cross-country—racing.

More quietly than a racing engine, but more powerful, something happened to forever change aviation. Something that was destined. The Commerce Department of the United States started laying down rules. And more than one man has suggested that those rules were the beginning of the end.

Especially for the barnstormers.

There were safety inspections, too rugged for a lot of the grizzled mechanical veterans of many hours and little rest. Then there were restrictions on areas of performance. And, like the gypsies Slats said they were, the barnstormers packed their gear and moved on.

But then the government people made their mistake.

They launched their second attack, this one on the air races themselves. And there they came up against business complexes which had contracts riding, like bets, on the races' outcome. They wouldn't be bullied. And, further, they supported the race promoters who wanted stunt, or precision flying teams as crowd-drawing attractions at their air races.

And, for as long as the races continued in their

importance, the businessmen continued in their victory.

But I said that stunt flying went in two directions.

One was Tommy Walker's way.

In 1946, after enough adventures to fill several lives, he came back to "barnstorming" and took Jack Hardwick's suggestion seriously. In May, he piloted an Aeronca C-2 at 65 miles an hour, skimming the ground at ten feet, and crashed into a wall of board and plaster. He got $1,000. And that was all right. He continued to log 23 deliberate crashes. In *Barnstorming* Martin Cadin continues the story by saying that Walker has a new idea. Now, he wants to do a head on crash at 50 feet with another plane. The FAA says it's suicidal. Walker evidently says something, too.

On the other road are flyers like Bevo Howard and Harold Krier. Howard came into it with a $100 plane, but as a businessman and a family man. And he took care of the craft. In 1938 he added his own stunt, the incredible outside loop. And he did it in a Piper Cub, less than a typical aerobatic machine. And as for Krier. Well, Cadin says he "brings even the old-time professionals to their feet in roaring applause for his exquisitely precise aerobatics." To me, he seems typified by his speech and mannerisms. He is a gentleman. And that is almost saying an anachronism. He flies because he "just had kind of a desire to do it." And he'll tell you truthfully that he doesn't "look at it as any different than any other job." And the distinction is more direct when he adds, "I never worked for anybody that wanted a danger show. . . . The whole secret is to be able to entertain without endangering other pepole, yourself or property."

And it is these precision aerobats—who don't like having their maneuvers termed stunts—who have seen their styles of flying become an international sport. Like most of the other minor sports, the United States arrived late. Krier recalls, "Americans were made aware of it in 1962 . . . when the U.S. participated as a team for the first time in Hungary." And the U.S. team was routed. They were, quite simply, far behind the times. The art had advanced quite highly in Eastern Europe, and even the scoring system was different. It was a different game than the national competition. But much about it remains the same.

In describing the Nationals, Krier catches the aspects of international competition, too.

"In contests everybody is flying the same routine, quite high and out of range . . . spectators come, but they don't know what they're watching . . . the contest is entirely a participant sport."

And it's tough and demanding. Imagine putting a plane through intricate turns, loops, spins, rolls and dives in a small invisible cube of air.

"The competition was always very serious. I entered to win." And Krier wasn't the only one. But he did win the Nationals in six of the years he entered, and retired from competition a champion.

"It was always a very hard week for me."

It would be a hard week for anyone. On the first two days, contestants fly the same plan of maneuvers. Then, on the last two days, one set that's handed them shortly before they go up, so there's no time for practice, and then sets they've prepared. And all the while the grading goes on.

Perhaps it was fitting that the 1964 international championship was held in Spain, because that new scoring system, the Aresti system, was developed by a Spaniard, and, as Krier puts it, "We arrived in Spain with zero knowledge about the book. We started out in their style of aerobatics about four years behind. We got a bad, late start."

But then how many people had even cared about aerobatics?

"A few years back," said Krier, "I could have named you every aerobatic pilot. Not any more."

It's changing.

Besides the grace, coordination and equipment what makes a champion? I don't know. But I know how rough it sounds as Krier continues, "I've practiced as much as anybody . . . practiced exactly like I was going to fly it at the contest. It takes total concentration . . . automatic reaction. In a contest you've got to be thinking of the maneuver you're flying and your placement and execution for three maneuvers beyond."

And if you see Krier in a show, he'll pull out his own maneuver, the Lomcevak, which translates into headache. Inverted, upside-down, he hangs, then starts his plane down, tumbling, rolling, end over end over end over end through the air. And try to imagine what it feels like, being pulled at and pushed by constantly shifting forces. And then he says, "Air shows have always been fun," and adds, in his still quiet voice, "It's enjoyable to fly for people who enjoy being entertained. In

all the years I've flown in the show, I've never seen a crowd that wasn't a good crowd. As a performer, I can actually feel it."

And maybe that's quite right, but I can't help but think that my generation of skywatchers are jaded. And part of the fun and beauty of the shows comes because the reality is filtered through distant memories of a different time. A different world. Perhaps it has become an attempt to be a conqueror among the colonists.

Antoine de Saint Exupery wrote in *Wind, Sand and Stars,*

Young barbarians still marveling at our new toys— that is what we are. Why else should we race our planes, give prizes to those who fly highest, or fastest? We take no heed to ask ourselves why we race: the race itself is more important than the object.

And this holds true of other things than flying.

For the colonial soldier who founds an empire, the meaning of life is conquest. He despises the colonist. But was not the very aim of his conquest the settling of this same colonist?

In the enthusiasm of our rapid mechanical conquests we have overlooked some things. We have perhaps driven men into the service of the machine, instead of building machinery for the service of man. But could anything be more natural? So long as we were engaged in conquest, our spirit was the spirit of conquerors. The time has now come when we must be colonists, must make this house habitable. . . .

In the end, it is always the men and the women who matter. And what they do and what is done to them. But even as they make their planes dance above the ground, seemingly unbelievable numbers of passengers are navigated through that same ocean of air. And, for me, when watching, there is no way to forget that. But what of conquerors

at a time when our civilization requires colonists? For them, their time is out of joint, their century is out of sync and they turn their conquest in and call it by a different name.

And it becomes—a sport.

In July 1971—the summer after I photographed him—Harold Krier died. He was killed as the airplane he test flew crashed. He was 49. The people who knew him well said that he was a gentleman and a kind man. And he was.

4
PARACHUTING

It's warm and there's a casual breeze coming in from the west. The small airplane flies in circles that lead higher and higher into the sky. Up there, over that large target, a man in a crash helmet holds a roll of yellow crepe paper. The plane's door is swung up and he leans, a little, out. The ground is far enough away to look unreal, as a series of lines and dots and splatters for roads, trees and ponds. It appears to be an excellent map. The pilot says, "Now." The paper drops out and unfurls. Wind carries it away from the plane and drops it gently down. That paper, called a wind-drift indicator, corresponds, somehow, to the fall of a hundred-pound man with a parachute. The pilot watches the streamer. Squinting through his dark glasses, he banks the craft and keeps going higher, but with a different sense of direction. He moves the plane in a way that carries it in a line from the marker as far from the target as the paper, but in the opposite direction.

Then, when the altitude is right, three men move forward. You can see the look in their eyes, the way their faces are. They are more than waiting. They are waiting with apprehension. But it is time.

They move to the door, a gaping hole in the airplane's side, and amble out. They hold onto the strut. Then the pilot says it again. "Now." And this time the men drop out. They seem to hang near the plane—then down. The fall is quick and they are only dots in seconds, and always dropping farther away.

From the ground, with very good eyes, or field glasses, you can see them climb out, hear the motor cut, and watch them fall, small frail things that can't seem human, falling—no not falling, it doesn't seem like a falling, not from the ground, the plane, or to them. It doesn't seem like falling—dropping, maybe. Like strange, heavy birds that have forgotten how to fly, or are just learning, they drop, down and down and down.

Then the crashing sound—a far off, soft explosion, as the parachute opens. The sleeve has pulled off, and the thin canopy streams above them, then it has filled with air and they hang, under that umbrella-looking thing. Now, they face into what wind there is and guide themselves in, into a position, close to what they had hoped for. There are a few people near the large Xed target, a photographer, in jeans and blue pullover, a girl-friend in jeans and striped shirt, a jumper in those high-soled black boots, and another in white short-sleeved shirt with a wife and a little blond-headed kid.

The other people are over nearer the packing shed, where the long narrow tables are draped with chutes being folded. And where the next set of jumpers are putting on orange, or blue, or black jumpsuits. And where one is looking for goggles because he's wearing contact lenses. A short, wild-haired man is puffing on a cigarette. That's Joe.

The wind pushes the paracommanders closer to the target, and the first chutist is smiling and

staring at the horizon to the North.

It's just about like this in a lot of America every weekend. A small field, a small plane, and a lot of parachutes. People have driven their cars and parked them on the turf and been flown up to jump out of an airplane more than a thousand feet over those cars.

And with it all the parachute has become a great big toy. Sure parachutes are still white, but they're also red and blue, black and gold, and I know a girl, Mia, who sports a shocking pink one.

All of this means that the parachute, like everything else I suppose, has come a long way from its tentative start, way back when.

The trouble is, nobody knows for sure when that when really was. But just to prove how much it's changed, look at the word. It comes from an Italian verb and a French noun which sort of mean: to guard against a fall. Now the idea is to make a fall possible. But, then, that idea is old, too. Supposedly Shih Huang Ti, a Chinese emperor in the latter part of the third century B.C., used some sort of parachute to jump off the then recently completed Great Wall. And that just shows how little world leadership has changed in a couple of thousand years. By the 14th Century, Chinese acrobats and actors were definitely using parachute-like devices in productions. All this, of course, was presumably unknown to Leonardo da Vinci who took a little time one day and designed a parachute. It was rigid and of pyramid shape and he called for linen in its manufacture. The

purpose to Leonardo? "... a man ... will be able to let himself fall from any great height without danger to himself." Evidently, a near contemporary of Leonardo's believed and may have toppled off a tower in Perugia without doing any great danger to himself.

Another Italian, Fausto Veranzio, had a problem. He became obsessed with parachuting before it existed in Western Civilization. In 1617 he put together a rigid canvas parachute and planned to jump off a tower in Venice. He didn't.

But who did? Well the Montgolfier boys, Joseph and Etienne, who made their reputation with balloons were testing parachutes with animals. For example in 1777 they tossed a sheep off a tower, which was probably quite a shock to the sheep. Sebastian Lenormand, a physics professor, fell off the Montpellier Observatory tower under a 14-foot canvas contraption and announced, shortly after arrival, that he'd just perfected a way of escaping from burning apartments. It didn't catch on. But something else did—his word. He coined the term parachute. Of course his thought was typical of the thought of these Western minds which made the chute an escape device—not an Emperor's toy.

A Frenchman was to start changing that, though. Andre Jacques Garnerin was whiling away his time in a Budapest prison designing parachutes. On October 22, 1797, he made what was probably the first sport parachute jump. Two thousand feet above a crowd of Parisian spectators, Garnerin stepped out of his balloon's basket and fell away under a spinning, oscillating wood and canvas

canopy that weighed more than a hundred pounds. He landed safely enough, but the shaking trip down was so rough, he got violently airsick on the way. His contribution to the parachute came because of that airsickness. He asked an astronomer friend how to keep the thing from oscillating. The advise was simple and direct. "Cut a hole in the top."

Soon there were a bunch of other firsts. A Pole made the first emergency jump, an American made the wildest—he allowed his balloon to explode at 13,000 feet and used it as his chute—and an Englishman died in a test jump with a rigid, linen parachute. Parachuting had truly become international. And it was only 1837.

Thomas Scott Baldwin, an American aeronaut, devised and introduced the first flexible, folded chute and developed a harness and shroud lines to go with it.

The modern parachute was taking shape. And other things were changing. There was still plenty of time for stunting daredevils to drop out of balloons at fairs. Parachutes were here. It was the balloons that were headed out.

It only took Charles Broadwick a few minutes after hearing of the Wright's first flight to realize that the chute as it existed was virtually worthless.

An airplane would be moving and there was no convenient place to hang a parachute. So in those lovely last years of innocence before the Great War, development went racing along.

E. R. Calthrop was starting on his Guardian Angel, Kathe Paulus was stuffing a chute in a sack that could be ripped open after she jumped. By 1908 there was a 25-pound parachute, in a pack with a rip cord, and it unfurled in about three seconds. It wasn't tried until 1912, though, when Arthur Lapham jumped from a Wright biplane. Previously, that same year, the first parachute jump from a moving airplane was logged in St. Louis, Missouri, by Captain Albert Berry.

It had been proven possible to drop out of an airplane and live to tell about it. But even airmen, who should have been a group of innovators, tended toward the conservative. They didn't want to bother with the strange, bulky things. Their biggest argument was that it would be too difficult to clear an airplane without fouling the chute. So when that war came parachutes were used sparsely. Observers in balloons tethered to the ground got them and some of them jumped more than half-a-dozen times in a given day. Magnesium flares got them, so they'd drift down slower. And spies got them—it was the start of the black parachutes—and were dropped behind enemy lines.

But it was late—1917—before one side became equipped with the lifesavers. German pilots carried them piled into a bucket in the plane. The American First Pursuit Group reported downing eleven planes and seeing the strange cloths flutter the German pilots to the ground. Before the war was over, all fliers would have them.

The war had lasted long enough. The parachute, as well as the airplane, had become legitimate. Neither would ever be quite the same again.

It was a spring day. Or what would pass for a spring day. But he was pure winter—coming toward us.

I lifted the field glasses from my eyes to get away from it—but I had to look back. He was in the sky and turning it into winter with white coveralls, a white parachute and a white-overcast sky. It was icy—watching him fall.

"Pull it to the left.

"Pull it to the left," Garrison said into the

motorola microphone and the words came out many times magnified.

Jim Garrison was lecturing a student and at the moment the only lesson was a little to the left.

Garrison had started jumping in 1959, and the little to the left lecture was coming in 1970. And he was still anxious for them, these newcomers, to experience what he'd experienced.

"It's a whole new world," he'd tell them.

And another student came twirling out of the plane; his static line pulled open the pack, but the chute was tangled around him, streaming back up, unfilled and unfillable with air. It was his first jump.

Mia was standing near the speakers by Garrison and me.

"Mister, open your chute. Open your chute. Why doesn't he open his chute?" she shouted into the wind. He kept falling, getting close, too close to the ground.

"I was touching my toes," he said, "trying to get the line free. . . . I took plenty of time. I wanted to make sure that went right."

"That" meant grabbing the D-ring on the emergency chest pack, pulling it, tossing the chute out and dropping under its canopy. He'd gone out of the plane wrong and tumbled over on top of his parachute.

And what about it?

"Yeah," he said, "I'll go back up."

And he walked, with his orange jumpsuit with the zippers up to the neck and the pockets attached in weird places and stood with the others who had jumped. For now, at least, a group a little separated from the rest of the world.

Matt Farmer was standing near the shed, smoking a Camel. He flipped his head to toss his long hair back out of his face. He watched the others walking around the area. It's old for Farmer. But that doesn't mean he doesn't love it. He was a gunner on a helicopter in Vietnam and one landing zone they used was held by air force elite who'd bribe a South Vietnamese helicopter pilot

with a couple of bottles of whiskey to take them up. They'd modified emergency chutes into sport jobs. They asked Farmer to come along.

"I wasn't doing anything on Sundays, and I wasn't worried about dying, so I joined them." For the next three years he spent every weekend at a drop zone. If the weather was too bad to jump, he'd pack chutes and talk. But he would be there. Maybe he always will.

But no matter where you get it, instruction is less casual than it used to be. Pilots didn't get any. You know, "What's the sense of practicing what has to be right the first time?" But neither did a lot of professional parachute jumpers. And there were a lot of professional jumpers in those crazy 1920s. Then, to have an air show all you needed were a couple of patched planes, a parachute, a little gas and a lot of guts. It lasted through those dangerous days and spilled into the next decade.

It was the depression and Tommy Walker was a 17-year-old kid. Right there with no luck and no work. But the word got around that some barn-

70

stormers needed a parachute jumper. Before evening Walker was one. But then he was going to be a lot of things in his time: air show ace, stuntman, parachutist, boxer, motorcycle racer, combat flier, soldier-of-fortune, smuggler, tramp, and a few other things you've always wanted to be. But his more than 350 jumps came off quite all right, with no instruction, save that first disgruntled pilot's gesture for "jump." Incidentally the delayed parachute jump openings that delighted crowds saved his life when he was shot down while flying in the Chinese Air Force. He held off on the rip cord until he reached 500 feet, and avoided the strafing that the Japanese then afforded bailed-out pilots.

He was special, but he was just one of hundreds of parachutists who crossed the country hunting adventure and money.

Another was Bonnie Rowe, a one-time smokestack painter and a wartime observer in captive balloons. Within a year after he was back from the war he'd built his reputation, and been among the first to hop from plane to plane. Only he'd done it with one hand tied behind his back. But doing it and making money at it weren't necessarily the same thing. As a free-lance photographer, I know how he felt.

In "Barnstorming" Martin Cadin tells one story about Rowe and money. Rowe was in and out of money so often he took to pawning his parachute to tide him over. One time it was in hock and he had a jump job, if he had a chute. He called a quick conference of his friends. They pooled their cash, and, even combined, it wasn't enough. That night, people kept sneaking into Rowe's hotel room with armloads of sheets and Rowe, turned seamstress, stitched together a canopy. The next day he jumped. The chute popped apart ten feet from the ground. He wasn't hurt.

Growing up with such stuntmen were the sport parachutists. At first they were limited to exhibitions of spot landing skill. Joe Crane lobbied for a competitive meet. He got his way when, in 1933, the National Aeronautic Association agreed and named him chairman of the parachute board.

The military wasn't overlooking parachutes either. General Billy Mitchell suggested "vertical envelopment," which meant dropping paratroopers behind enemy lines. It wasn't a totally original idea. Napoleon had considered it and Ben Franklin

had conjured up something like that when he suggested that ". . . 10,000 men descending from the clouds, might . . . in many places, do an infinite amount of mischief before a force could be brought together to repel them." And on a smaller scale it's hinted at in ancient African legends.

In the 1930s, sport parachuting became a regular activity in the Soviet Union. In 1933, the first sport jump school was established, there, and graduated 1,200 persons the same year. All across the countryside there were airplane jumps and, to supplement them, specially constructed jump towers. Within three years there were at least 21,000 sport, free-fall jumps. That number increased vigorously until the Second World War cut the whole thing short.

Not surprisingly, the Soviet Union was the first nation to use paratroops in war. Not that the other powers weren't equipped, but the USSR had an early opportunity in the 1939–40, Russo-Finnish conflict.

Of course the world war would contribute to other changes and modifications of parachute uses. But mostly what it would do was end, and let

loose a lot of people who had a taste for action that wouldn't quit with a surrender.

By 1949, sport jumping was a big thing in France. The government established ten subsidized training areas. A year before that the *Féderation Aeronautique* Association had established the International Parachute Commission. And by 1954 the U.S. had entered its first international meet. More or less. Actually one jumper went and competed single-handedly against the five-man teams representing the other countries. Such contests judge two areas—style and precision. The style concerns how well the jumper performs maneuvers during free-fall, the precision how close he comes to the center of the target on landings. Incidentally, the U.S. loner was Fred Mason.

The next year a Frenchman, again, was to change things. And it would all happen by accident. Jacques André Istel was just flying over Illinois when his plane developed troubles. He crashlanded in a farm field, but decided to be better prepared for a next time. He hunted up Joe Crane and told him he wanted to learn how to jump. That did it. Within a year he was a representative from the U.S. (he was a naturalized citizen) to the International Parachute Commission conference in Vienna. On his way home he detoured through Paris and had Sam Chasak, the French national champion, teach him how to sky-dive. Then he came back and put together a team to represent the U.S. They rated sixth out of ten. But Istel was just starting. He quit his lucrative Wall Street job and turned his attention, full-time, to sky-diving. He threw together Parachute, Inc., at Orange, New Jersey, and started teaching all comers how to jump and sky-dive. His original idea for simple, relatively cheap training centers spread across the country.

In the 1960 contests the U.S. finished fourth.

In 1962, the U.S. with an all-Army team took first. In the 1920s Major E. L. Hoffman had led a group of test-jumpers in developing a chute for the Army. By the early 1960s, the Army had their own elite parachute performers, The Golden Knights. Oh yes, the times had changed.

But seeing contests and exhibitions isn't what this is all about. You could paraphrase Phil Edwards's "Surfing is for kicks, not crowds," and catch the meaning just fine.

It's late afternoon, now, and the day is hot and dusty. Three or four people are sitting on the edge of a packing table, just in the shade of the shed. They're waiting for their turn to climb up into the sky and let go. Most of these people are in their early twenties and go to college. Not all. One man, older than the others, has log books that list well over three hundred jumps, and he goes at it lightly. He learned in the 1950s.

He props a foot onto the little table and his toe touches a helmet.

"Yeah, I started quite a while ago. Where I lived . . . I could look out my front-room window and watch these guys jump every Sunday afternoon.

"I was working in a sporting goods store at the time, and one came in. He had a little patch on his jacket and I started talking to him. I told him I'd like to jump sometime. So he gave me his address and told me to come over that night. And we went out and jumped."

"No training, no nothing?" asks one of the college kids.

"Nothing."

"They didn't even tell you to face into the wind?"

"They used to tell you to do the wrong thing, and then laugh at you. Crazy. Just crazy."

He lit a cigarette and went on to tell about his big exhibition jump. He was scheduled to fall into a Missouri airport, and he dutifully left the plane, free-fell a little, then pulled the rip cord to maneuver right onto the runway.

"I stood there, the smoke cans still hot in my hands, waiting for the applause. But there wasn't any applause. Hell, there wasn't any crowd. I'd jumped into the wrong airport."

It had to come to that, the question was waiting to be asked.

"I'm not like the rest of these guys. I'm a coward. And I'm the first one to admit it. It scares me. Every time, it scares me.

"But I think we all like to be scared. Good and scared. And come out of it."

You'll get different answers—as you ask that "why?"—from different people. Joe tipped me off to it though. He'd been out of the service for six years when I met him, and he spent his weekends at a drop zone, jumping as much as he could. The rest of the week he stood in an assembly line. "Hell, I can go to work, and not be awake for the first four hours and it wouldn't make any difference," he said.

But the weekends. Ah, that was something else. Dropping, there's a silence, a ruffle of wind, a need for firm concentration, a being scared, an experience of flying, an exhilaration, an exhaustion, a sense of individual supremacy, an understanding, a—a feeling. Simply a feeling.

To feel. Sure that's what it's all about.

In a world where a "civilized" man can live the majority of a lifetime without truly feeling, it suddenly becomes more important than only just living.

There's a relatively new parachute. It appeared in a sport model late in 1969. It's called a wing and looks like a large kite. It's taken from F. M. Rogallo who envisioned a large, inflatable model for space capsules. The sport parachutists beat him to it.

You watch somebody bring one down, cork-screwing it to the ground, being flung around and

around, being the weight on the end of the lines. "It's like flying," Bruce Brown tells you and you look at it—a red, white and blue triangle looking more like a kite every minute.

And you know it. They and that long-time-ago Chinese emperor have found something that had been worth looking for. And they've found it in one of the danger sports.

You know I hate, detest, and can't bear a lie, not because I am straighter than the rest of us, but simply because it appalls me. There is a taint of death, a flavour of mortality in lies—which is exactly what I hate and detest in the world—what I want to forget. It makes me miserable and sick, like biting something rotten would do. Temperament, I suppose—Joseph Conrad

5
KARTING

The smoke pours up, almost white, and heavy. Clouding the air just above the ground, the smoke covers all with its haze and the noise is harsh and grating and grabbing, as the engines unwind. The smoke pours up and the noise fights it for control and a man stands poised beside the railing with the flags in his hands. The engines are all started and the race is beginning, soon they'll be away from the rail and fighting for a shot down the straightaway. Then there's the moving into the first turn and it is really begun. Then, for an hour, it goes on—seeing who can last to win—piling up the most miles before the sixtieth minute has run through its last second. Then it is over; the passing, the praying, the running, and turning and cornering are finished for them and their set of small machines; then the track is quiet as the sound like the buzzing of great bees is dead and stays dead—until the next race; then that race has been run, and there is nothing but the notification of winners.

Sixty minutes. That's all. And that's what it's all about. The work, the worry, the travel, the engine tuning, and body design are all built into that hour. Now it is the big hour. It is the hour that separates the national enduro champion from the ones who also ran. So it is here they come to try for trophies. It is here they come to race their low platforms on small slick tires. It is here they come.

But, compared to other motor racing sports, they haven't been coming for long. You can trace the ancestral line of these 1970 International Kart Federation nationals to their birth—to 1959 and Azuza, California. There they came to race in their championships on the first track built for go-karts. And then, karts hadn't even existed for long, just four years.

It was 1955, Art Ingels and Lou Borelli were living in Echo Park, California. Ingels was working on Quarter Midget Racers for Kurtis Kraft in Los Angeles. He and other employees chased each other through the parking lot in those bodyless midget cars and Ingels thought—just thought—it might be fun, sometime, to build a little car that way.

In a seemingly unrelated incident, the McCulloch Corporation, which was then making lawn mowers, decided to change engines and were stuck with a few thousand West Bend motors. So they started selling off the two-cycle engines at $14 a piece.

Now Ingels had an idea and an engine. He and Borelli tinkered until they had a prototype. Then they made more. Soon their little cart-like contraptions were attracting attention and seemed to some a splendid way of having fun.

And there was really only one thing to do with them—race. And almost instantly karts spread to the East, then rapidly, back across the middle west.

The Go-Kart Manufacturing Company made the machines and gave them a name which stuck. It gave the drivers a club, too, to sanction races and establish rules. The Rose Bowl parking lot and other, less sporty but equally open, asphalt areas became prime targets for short-distance sprint tracks.

Fathers bought the little machines almost as toys for their sons. Then, discovering a speed and maneuverability which delighted, fathers reclaimed the same little machines and raced them. The time finally came, when, if you were a cinemastar, you simply had to be photographed taking a go-kart through a turn—or at least sitting on one.

In the early 1960s, it all looked too good to last.

It was.

Karting prospered in those years. Enduros were begun. These longer races appealed to a different type of driver. But they appealed. And soon they needed their own national championship meets. They had the first one in Ft. Worth in 1963. Each race lasted an hour and a half and was run over a sports car track.

By the mid-Sixties, though, the glamor had

started to dissolve. Some people dropped out of the sport, but those who stayed were serious. And, from that time until these nationals in 1970, it's been racing for the racers.

And with the racers come the engine, and body and special fuel makers, and the correspondents from their magazine and the officials from their federation. When you notice this, you know you're in a very special, closed-circuit society—a separate world. But the sport has built up from the inside as people came to play, and stayed.

They stay for their own reasons.

Some will tell you they're frustrated automobile racers. That this is maybe the cheapest racing around. That they started when they were fifteen, and what else could they race? But they stay with it. And they tell you about their own special hero —Mickey Rupp. Rupp left kart racing for a year

and, through connections, skill and ambition wound up on the Indianapolis Speedway track during a 500-mile race. He finished sixth, then came back to karting. Others want to go. Others like Nationals' winner Chuck Pittenger. Pittenger, in 1970, had raced for 13 of his 25 years and says he'd like to leave karts for a pro driver's spot on the USAC circuit. He's not the only one looking in that direction.

But, in finding many of their heroes in different racing machines, karters might overlook the candidates in their midst. And they've got plenty. Some with the stuff that legends are made of. All a part of the sport and a piece of its puzzle.

There's George Cardas, for example. His hair is long, his voice is soft and he's tall enough to look down on most people. A few years ago he was in the construction business, had extra time

and money and wanted something to do besides work.

"I'd raced years ago," he said, "and remembered how much fun it was."

Back in, on the fringes, Cardas followed a friend to the track. "He always ran a strong second. So I mixed him up a little something and he annihilated them." Now, as you walk along the pits, the red cans seem almost everywhere—red cans with little white labels that read "Cardas Racing Fuels T4 Alky."

And from New York there's Lou Smiley, appreciably older than Cardas's 24 years, but having an ageless quality about him. When I talked to him, he was operating a kart shop, was very involved with the peace movement in the United States, and was editor and publisher of an underground newspaper. He raced for fun, and meant it when he said that racing—even if for last place—with another driver was enough to make it all worthwhile.

His is a one-man operation. And some say that sort of karting is dying. It was Cardas who told me, "No longer will a single individual effort be enough. No longer will one man win alone." He paused. "Which means, it's a pro sport."

John Beaver is a welder in Los Angeles. He races enduro karts. His wife, Ginger, races sprints. They were driving past a race track when they saw the little machines moving. They wondered what they were. When they found out, they made it their sport. But now, they'll tell you, it's gotten expensive. They have no team. For them and their charming daughter, JoAnn, this is part of their vacation.

Traditionally, karting was labeled a family sport. And everyone could race, and come, and maybe have a picnic, and a good time. By 1970 that was still quite true at local sprint tracks, but a good enduro needed a sports car track and racers from a long way off—something that makes it more serious, less casual. Then there's kart design, which changes every few years, and engines which need constant attention. It could quickly become more work than fun. And if it's going to be work, you might as well get paid for it. The factory team racers do—not for the racing, but for the products they sell which have been promoted through the racing.

Bob Allman is one of these. Sometimes they

call him Mr. Clean. At the end of a day in the pits, his tee shirt and white jeans will be less black than the others. After a practice run, or a race, he'll be back in the pits, rags in hand, wiping down his machine.

"Sometimes if there's any malfunction, you find it. You're always finding things that are loose . . . just by cleaning your equipment."

As he polishes the already bright fuel tanks, Allman, in his mind, is sorting out the rough spots of this track. He probably doesn't think about how it all began for him. About how he was lifeguarding in Hawaii, and how there was a track and rentable go-karts that delighted him then, and how when he came back to the mainland and discovered racing karts he knew what he wanted to do. He's made karting his business and races on the Inglewood Kart Supply Team—which is *not* a one man effort. The new kart he stands polishing was not a one man effort. But Allman is quite responsible for its design. He's big and karts are awfully small. Using every inch of length, he can slink low for that nearly prone position most enduro racers demand to cut wind resistance. It's going to be this kart's big go, too. It's an American Reed machine, and that stock engine class was new at these 1970 nationals. Allman's wife stayed home. For him it is a business trip.

Next to Allman, in the pits, is Gary Hartman. He comes in limp, looking wet and ragged and tired and entirely too hot, after taking his practice laps. Now, with his leathers and crash helmet off, he sits, sipping Gatorade and mistaking a hot breeze for a cool one. The others on the team

gather around as he tells them some of what he's learned about the track. This Hartman makes the sport seem older than it is. He's second generation. Across the open area there's another team—the Hartman team, but he's not on it. There is John Hartman, one of the sport's old men. He also runs a karting concern—Hartman Engineering. With him is his wife, Kathey, his top racer in a racing game that doesn't push women into separate classes. John's son, Gary, grew up around kart racing engines and looked like a champion for sure until—Vietnam. He took too many machine-gun slugs in his arm and some of the doctors wanted to amputate. When the kart racers heard about it, they thought it was all over for him. One racer didn't. That was Gary. Oh, the arm hangs a little limp and carries a sizable scar, but he can push a kart around the course. And this time he'll have something to prove, to others, and to himself.

Now, though, he sits, sipping the Gatorade and talking about the track and how it should be run.

And then it's Thursday and hot and race day, and the people sit with their karts underneath the awnings. They sit and work on the engines and clutches and hope it will come out all right for them. The day is bright and clear and the light from the sun is splattered over everything. The early race karters push their karts into the pre-grid, then down and onto the track and in the middle of the long straightaway. There, according to number, they line them against the guard railing, angling them only so slightly to the left, to the track.

The drivers meet with the race director. He's supposed to go over the rules. Some use that time, too, to put on gauze facemasks or tie bandanas—bandit style—over their mouths. Then, back by their karts, they put on their naugahide motorcycle jackets and pants or chaps, and their helmets and then they sit down, so low, into those karts.

Suddenly it's time for the engines to be started, and they start with a sputter from the portable

starters, then cough up their sweet, almost white smoke to make a low cloud all along the line.

The flagman signals their release from the wall and off they run, in a sound of acceleration, a shift of smoke and a confusion of getting into the open.

Around the course, they go, spreading out before the turns, taking them, someone passing, almost always, passing or coming into position to pass. Around the course and into the pylon-narrowed scoring turn where official timers clock their procession and mark their laps ended. Into it, slower, and going single file then moving and trying to get more speed to go back down that straightaway, and past the position where they started and where their friends or family or team members keep their clocks and lap charts and starters and spare parts, and best wishes. So the hour is begun,

and so it will go with karts constantly moving around the same course, through the same turns, down the same straights, with drivers remembering the track and how they want to run it—flat-out fast—and keeping that speed up and trying to win.

And maybe the race that's started is B-American Reed. So Smiley and Beaver and Allman are all out there—with 51 others. So it's hot—damned hot.

So Smiley's kart can't keep it up, and he brings it in after a few laps.

So Beaver keeps going, but Allman is going stronger. Stronger than any of the others as the day gets even hotter.

Through the turns and rattling rapidly into the straights, and Allman is passing. Allman in the black racing leathers, of IKS, Beaver in his own jacket and chaps. And the heavy hard, but high

and piercing sound goes on until the checkered flag flips up at the scoring turn to signal the end.

Into the straightaway, but slower, much slower now, and stopping to turn off the track and go into the weigh-in compound.

The karts are already stacked up behind the scales; drivers are waiting to get a chance to weigh-in and get out. There must be at least 350 pounds there. Allman comes in, and stops his kart to the side of the line waiting, and sits, uneasily and briefly in the now quiet racer. Then, still slowly, he lifts himself up, and stops. Then off comes the masking helmet. His hair is wet, his eyes squint at the sun.

A little to the east, in Indianapolis, the temperature is setting a record by nestling one notch under a hundred, and here in Clermont on the Indianapolis Raceway Park track it's hotter. Allman, and now Beaver as he comes in, feel it.

Allman is nearly exhausted and the heat hits him hard when he stops. It hits them all hard when they stop. It's there on the track, but there is wind, and it's not so noticed—there's not the feeling of sweat running down your body, and a real knowledge that you are too hot. That comes, and hits hard, when you stop. It almost knocked Allman out. Later, in his motel room, he said he felt, several times, that he was going to pass out, out there after that race. But he didn't. And when he'd weighed in, and they'd inspected his kart and found no violation, he became his race's winner.

Beaver came off the track looking a little better. But when I asked him how he felt, he passed the question by and put his palms over his ear.

"The goddamned mufflers fell off and I can't hear a fucking thing."

He shook his head a couple of times and then

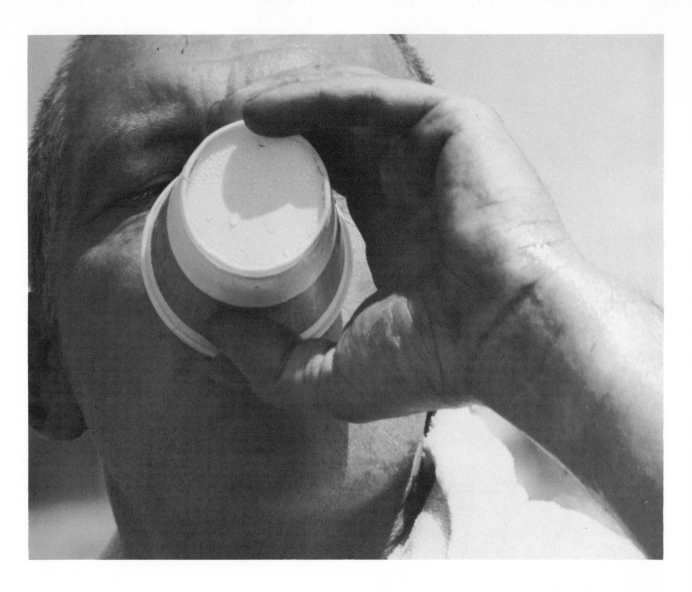

moved closer. "Look at this," he held up his left hand, the tip of his index finger was ripped apart.

"How the hell did you do that?"

"I guess I stuck it in the flywheel when I was tuning," he said, "Hey, do we have to stay here? I've got to get some water. Jesus."

He found someone with water and got a sip, then stood waiting. Finally Ginger came with a plastic bottle full of the stuff.

An IKS man handed Allman a bottle of Gatorade and he tried drinking it.

Then the other races have been run and the day is over and those who are going back into Indianapolis go, and those who have come to camp, camp. And in motel pools, tired racers splash through cool waters.

Tomorrow is a different day.

It would be a different day, in several ways.

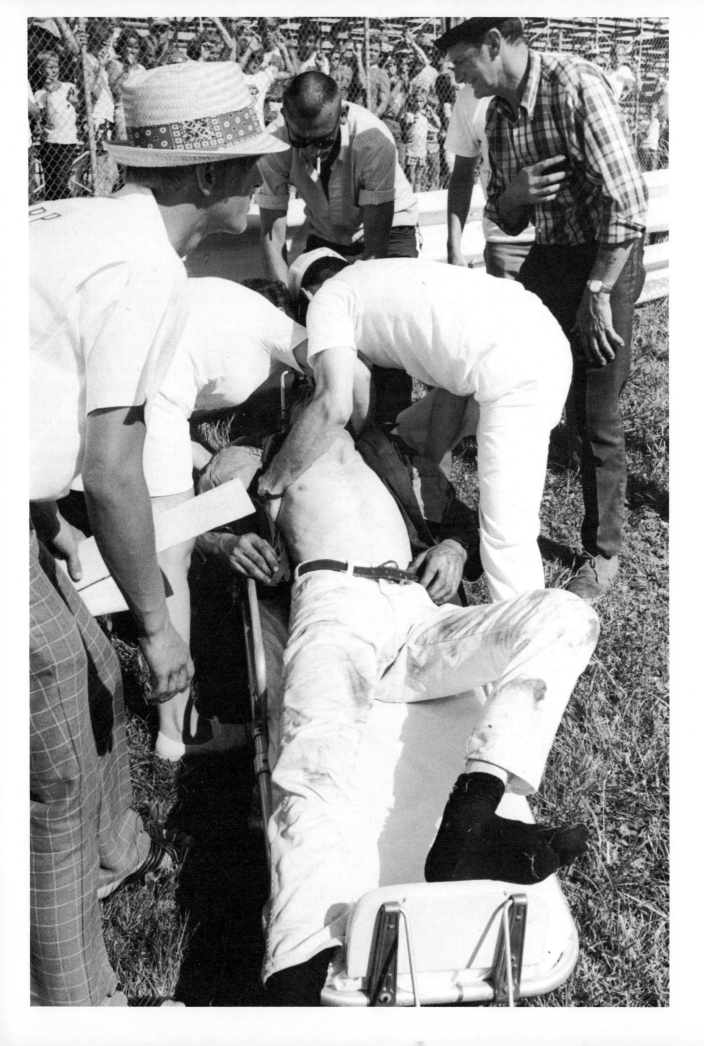

First, there was some rain, and a cover of clouds occasionally masked the sun. Not too often, though. Gary Hartman was looking happier, just as pleasant, but more confident after his win the day before. And this day progressed, as the others, with racers racing. Soon it was time for the FKEs. These initialed classes are new in a sport where nothing is very old. The letters stand for formula kart enclosed, and the bodies are strange in shape and size. There is no limit on engine price and modifications, and unlike the bodiless karts they may have gear-boxes. Most use motorcycle engines.

First on the program were FKE IIIs, the biggest. They were running with B-Open. I was standing off a series of S curves, photographing the karts as they came through. When I was done, I wanted to go back to the impound area and see the drivers coming off the track. I hitched a mini-bike ride with another cameraman. On the way, some official shouted and pointed toward an ambulance and a downed driver. We went over. I jumped off the back of the bike and ran closer. In the quick, easy, reflex way you develop, I shot off a few frames of the ambulance company working with him, getting him on the stretcher and preparing to move out. At the same time the high-race official came hurrying across the grass and jumped the guardrail near me, shouting at me to cut it out, to stop.

He insisted that I couldn't take any pictures of that. Obviously, since I had, I could. He demanded my film.

"You want the film? Well, get a court order and try to get it."

We stared into each other's sunglasses, as he demanded the film, and why I'd taken that shot. He got nowhere. So finally he drew himself up to full height and said,

"Well, let me tell you this, buddy, it's a long straight road. . . ."

"Yeah? Is that supposed to mean something?"

The scene ended, a few minutes later, in the track tower when I still refused to hand over the film and complained about the treatment. So I was ordered off the track. The reason for the expulsion was never terribly clear, but it appears to spring from a notion that such a photograph would damage the image of kart racing. But in fact, it says that all the news is never fit to print, only the part you want. Significantly, the part that isn't wanted isn't wanted because it appears to those with power to alter their otherwise favorable image. But instead of altering the facts to make them all favorable, the concern is always with altering the spread of the news of the facts. There are such officials everywhere.

Unfortunately, some have real power—not four-day-duration-of-race power.

He remembered poor Julian and his romantic awe of them and how he had started a story once that began, "The rich are different from you and me." And how someone had said to Julian, Yes, they have more money. But that was not humorous to Julian.—Ernest Hemingway

6
POLO

It was raining before I ever got there.

The rain started in downstate Illinois and I drove through it and through the fog-mist that it became farther north and finally came back into the Sun. I listened to the WLS broadcasted weather reports and heard how the rain and chill would be gone and the weekend would be hot and like summer again, but I knew that was not true.

It was the start of September and it was fall.

And I felt that, and it was true.

I was still thinking about that when, under sun, I drove into the Oakbrook International Sport Core compound. The road was paved but narrow, and the trees ran up on both sides of the road. They were still very green, but the time of day—late afternoon—and the denseness of the trees made them dark and mysterious the way a magical forest is supposed to be.

I drove until I came to a fork in the road. There were two men mowing grass between the roads. I stopped my car and asked where the polo clubhouse was.

"¿Polo?," the younger one asked the other, "¿que es polo?"

"Polo," I answered him, "*es un juego. Los caballeros juegan polo. Ocho caballeros.*" And not trusting this, added descriptive moves.

"*¿Pero,*" I said, "*no conoce donde es? ¿Donde esta la casa de los hombres de polo?*"

The older one told me through words and pointing, and I drove along the now gravel road until I saw what looked like a movie set mansion with a vast, slightly up-sloping lawn leading toward the great brick eminence. I drove around it, stopped the car and sat looking at the place. Brick, big, heavy white columns and looking exactly as if it belonged off this gravelled road, surrounded by that magnificently green grass, and the deeper evergreen shrubbery that stood up close to it.

Then I started the car.

I couldn't take the inside now, it would wait until morning.

The two men were still mowing away at the grass as I drove my rattling Dodge past them.

"*¿Que es polo?,*" I thought. And I knew it was more than a game.

As for me, when I think of polo I think of the British Army and India. The long, hot, Indian day, then, as Churchill reflects, "the evening shadows proclaimed the hour of Polo. . . ." But India, and that British Army of Empire, came late in a game that kings and emperors had been a long time breaking in. The game had moved, with Mohammedan conquerors, from Persia into

India in the 1200s. By the late 16th Century, it had achieved prominence. Akbar the Great became its champion and equipped his ten-man teams with golden sticks. Akbar himself, though, was late in that line of men-of-power polo players. It was a favorite sport of Chinese Emperors at least as early as 709 A.D. And also in China, it truly became a danger sport. Emperor T'ai Tsu watched a favorite relative die in a match in 910 and promptly ordered all participants beheaded.

This early Chinese polo, like the early Greek and Japanese style, was played differently than the Arabian, Indian and contemporary types. The Chinese played the ball into nets rather than between goalposts and, in one variation, the ball went up at the beginning of the game and was not supposed to drop until it hit the nets in a score. The glamor and pageantry associated with the game then was, evidently, a spectacle almost beyond belief. Horses were covered with feathers, bells, mirrors and other fancy stuff, and saddles might well be fitted out with jewels.

The game finally fell out of favor in China though and was finally dropped in the Manchu, the last, Chinese dynasty.

The Arabians, who eventually moved the game into India, had learned it in Persia and watched it become a pleasure of caliphs and sultans. Harun-al-Rashid so loved his polo that his son set out a full course inside a Baghdad castle. By the way, part of the Mohammedan success in defeating the continuous Crusaders of the Middle Ages is attributed to their cavalry tactics and mounts—both seasoned, perhaps, in the lesser battles of the polo field.

But it all goes back to Persia. And, for a long time, those historians who've messed with the subject credit the Persians with originating the

If these Iranians were the first masters of the horse that probably catches it; if not, someone else may push the beginnings of polo back even farther. But about two thousand years is a pretty good run for any sport. And it's got that.

It has something else, too. A position that no other sport won or held for nearly as long. It was a pastime for rulers. From Sassanian sovereigns, through emperors and sultans up to its twentieth-century standing among princes, ex-rajas and millionaires, polo belonged to the ruling class. It slipped, for a moment, in the 1800s when it became a common sport among the hillsmen of the upper Indus valley. The British Army, though, changed that when they brought it, through themselves, back to the rulers.

It wasn't all that early the next day, when I finally got back to that polo house and stopped the Dodge in the parking lot. I walked up the paved drive and opened one of the weathered doors. Inside it was dark and cool and looked old and worn, the way a country shooting coat is

sport. It certainly existed there, and early. In the epic poem *Shahnameh* there runs the line,

> At seven years old he went upon the ground
> To learn the art of war and play at polo.

The boy was Sapor II, a ruler in the land. And, supposedly, polo was quite a national sport there as early as the third or fourth century A.D. Women and men both played. The game wove itself into the art of the times, and the lives of the people.

Now Berthold Laufer insists that polo goes back beyond its time in Persia. He suggests that it was originated by the Iranian Tribesmen in the heart of Asia, in the first or second century A.D. He also says that, there, it was much less the game than the training exercise and was offered along with swordsmanship and archery as required courses for the soldier. This whole theory seems proper when you consider that these Iranian groups have already been described as the first domesticators of horses, and credited as the creators of cavalry.

91

supposed to look. Tables were being laid out for a lunch and a couple of Mexican-Americans were moving around the room carrying glasses and plates. I looked over the paintings. Above the fireplace was a massive portrait which held the room at bay. It featured Paul Butler, a favorite horse and white Persian cat. The cat looked fat. Butler didn't. Down from that, and to the left, was a flashing, colored blur of the action that is polo. I guessed, then checked for Leroy Neiman's signature. It was there. And I would remember it again, clearly, when I thumbed through a copy of *Esquire* and came face to face with Neiman in a whiskey advertisement. Neiman's statement said that man reveals himself best in his pleasures— the fun and games and fashionable distractions. In these areas of less pretense his problems become most obvious.

A couple of days later, if you asked the players, the most obvious problem was rain. The rain came and stayed and made the grounds—already watered—too wet to play. It stayed that way through the first two days of scheduled matches, Labor Day and the Sunday before it. The polo watchers who had come in from Virginia, California, France, England and other distant spots, left the Chicago suburb of Oakbrook without seeing a game, and the field watchers at the Sports Core waited until Wednesday before proclaiming the course dry enough to play.

Wednesday was a beautiful day. The moisture had cleared out the air, and the sun settled down, giving even light and not too much heat.

Sonny Le Jeune was standing down near a set of stables. Someplaces he'd be called a farrier. In Illinois the license says, simply, Horse Shoer. He's a jockey who grew up.

"But I like horses, and that's the only way I can make a living with them," he said. He stopped now, resting a bad back and waiting for a hand to bring the next horse up. For the most part he'll use shoes that come out of a box. They can be the same shoe you'd put on any other horse, but some of the players like a lighter weight model. They get those. And a pony can get a new set about every three weeks. It's not that the shoe wears down, but the hoof grows out around it and needs trimming.

The horses were fed at about six in the morning. They'll miss their noon meal and be on the playing field at about 3:00. Before that they get all the water they want, then stand by, late in the afternoon, to get their legs wrapped. That's simple protection against being hit by a ball or mallet. They'll probably be trucked over to the field and walked back. Before they leave the stables, about four will be saddled and bridled to ride. The others will be saddled and bridled during the match and standing ready for later periods of play.

They're beautiful horses, as you'd expect. Some had a go at the racetrack. Some never had a chance. There is no one breed best suited to polo. There is no polo pony. In fact, the term pony is inappropriate, and some suggest it caught on when Welsh ponies and other smaller breeds were played in Great Britain. The idea of a string of ponies came because riders need a fresh mount for each period and that makes six. Most of the serious players have at least seven horses ready to play. And each horse, when he's playing, can be worth as much as a very fully equipped automobile. It takes between one and two years, usually, to train a horse to play, and there's about a fifty percent dropout rate. But some of the ones who make it go beyond being polo ponies and become almost legendary figures in the sport. In the United States there have been, among others, Prince Friarston, Jupiter and Buena Vista.

When Jupiter was sold, incidentally, the price was $22,500.

Harold Barry is big, outdoors Texas tough. He's waiting for the game, too. Propped against a dusty pickup truck he rolls a cigarette and sets it on fire. He sums up the importance of the horse to the game at least as well as anyone else when he says, "If you can't get there, you can't hit the ball." And Barry ought to know about polo and horses. He runs horses on his Texas ranch, and he's been rated a nine-goal player since the second half of the 1950s. Ten-goal is the highest possible mark. Those ratings are awarded by the United States Polo Association and are based on the player's horsemanship, value to the team, hitting, understanding and handling of his team position and the quality of his horses, plus a near catchall of "Game Sense." This game sense attempts to evaluate his understanding of the game as it is being played, and so includes his anticipation of plays, building plays, general moves and strategy. The handicapping process started in the States

very shortly after the game was introduced here. In addition to classing players it equalizes matches. For example, this U.S. Open is a twenty-goal tournament, which means each four man team must have a combined rating of, at least, twenty goals. I should tell you that goal, used here, has no relation to the use of goal as a score. The word was applied and has stuck. It's just a term for the unit rating of the handicap, though.

Barry would be playing with the Tulsa team in this match, and his nine goals made him their top rated player.

"When it's over you might be a little dehydrated . . . it's a little strenuous," he took a drag on his cigarette, "you work up a sweat at it."

And you want to know how tough it is.

"Well," he says, "you can make it as rough as you want to."

And you know what he means. You also know that it's not just a young man's sport. Barry, for example, has been playing for longer than I've been alive.

"It's not like other sports. You don't use your legs. The falls are harder on your shoulders and the upper part of your body." So it figures you don't have to give up because your legs go bad. But it is even stronger than that.

"A fellow that's played a hell of a lot has got experience. And it's just hard to play enough to get that when you're still young."

The problem with getting older, here, is that your reflexes slow, and that takes the edge off your game.

And, you wonder, do you have to get up for a polo game?

"Yeah. You get up for it and you get your horse up to the peak, too. We've had four or five bad days . . . and we got to get them back up.

And you have to guess at it because those horses don't do much talking.

"Horses got a hell of a lot to do with the game. You start with the horses. . . . And if you have a spirited horse you wish they all were."

How long is a horse good for, when do they quit? You want to know.

"Fifteen, sixteen, seventeen years, maybe," he says and throws away his cigarette. "The life of a polo pony is his damn legs."

"Why do you play?"

"Why?"

"Yes, sir."

"It's fun," he says straight out. "Yeah. You can't beat it. Sure, it's fun. It's great sport."

I moved off, then after a little turned to look back at Barry. He had his windbreaker off now and was walking along the stables. A massive man in a khaki shirt, faded, soiled jeans tucked in knee high western boots and a well worn Stetson. Sometimes it's too easy to forget that there are people like that still around.

Barry was one of the others.

If you run into a good polo player, ask him

how he keeps in shape, and he'll probably tell you that he rides almost every day. Usually that's in the morning. Now to have that time, and access to your horses, you've just about got to be a man who can order his own time—which includes the very leisure class—or it's got to fit into your work. Well Barry raises horses, and polo is a lot of his life. He's a professional. And I think the distinction between the two types, truly does mean something.

Sonny was still shoeing. A polo player was leaning against his station wagon and watching.

"You don't have a bad back?"

"Well, yes, I do," the player said, and explained.

"I don't see how you shoe your horses. It just about kills me," says Sonny.

"Well I don't shoe them all anymore. I just shoe my pet."

Sonny was looking at a hoof, his hammer poised above the nail.

"Who shoes the rest?"

"My Mexicans," the player says.

Sonny hits the nail. The conversation is, it seems, over.

Up at that green trailer, which serves as headquarters for these polo matches, Marion Hopkins is telling telephoners that, yes, today there really will be a game. Just off that office area there are a couple of burlap bags full of the white bamboo balls. A polo ball is lighter than I'd expected. It should weigh between 4 1/4 and 4 3/4 ounces and be about 3 1/2 inches in diameter. And that ball is the target the player has to hit, while he's riding on about half a ton of horse, and racing perhaps forty miles an hour toward it. And all of this happening on a field 150 yards wide and 300 yards long with a goal eight yards wide and ten feet tall.

A gray-haired man walked into the trailer and checked times for the matches. I asked him if he'd played. He seemed happy for the question and said he had played in college, then in the Army. He looked like an officer out of someone's past—not tall, but so properly groomed and so—what other word can you use—very properly dressed.

"When they mechanized the cavalry in 1942 they did away with the horses. . . . That did away with the polo. . . . But before, we had low bills:

no stabling, no veterinarians, no grooms. . . . it was like we were millionaires," he said.

But if polo was going to end in the Army, perhaps that was the time to end it. It had reached its height in the United States during the 1930s. The uprise started in the late 1920s, and climbed through the depression. Tommy Hitchcock was riding high, and he was one ten-goaler whom the old aficiondos will tell you made light of a rating scale that stopped that low. In those days, Devereux Milburn was the great grand old man of the game. His fame had started when the century did. He played with Harry Payne Whitney, Larry and Monty Waterbury in a team that did for polo what Knute Rockne did for football.

That was part of America's contribution to the game; another was altering the British eight-man teams to four, which is where it still stands.

And the mechanizations of the cavalry marked a fitting date for the final wops of mallet on ball because it formalized the different directions war,

101

and the world, were taking. It is no coincidence that George Patton built his legend as a commander of men in machines. And during the Battle of the Bulge, Patton brought his staff together and told his subordinates that "All you've got to use, is brains and guts. That wins polo games and it wins battles."

Cecil Smith is another Texan. He kept a ten-goal rating for a quarter of a century. He dropped out, not to quit, but until he can get his injured hand back in shape. He talked to me about what it used to be like to play, and part of what he said was, "More people had money in those days and spent more money than they can now. You don't have that kind of people anymore. But there's more polo than ever."

Part of why there is more polo is because, in Ohio, a group of people who you'd think would be going to the closest pro football game on Sundays got together and made their own field, and left an old barn standing to serve as a cheap clubhouse.

Two thousand years is a long time. And what seemed important now was a game that was finally going to get underway. It was a semifinal match; the winner would go on to play for the National Open Championship—and an unbelievably ornate trophy with this unbelievably ornate inscription: "Presented by Joseph B. Thomas as a perpetual challenge trophy for the competition of the world."

It would be a beautiful afternoon for a piece of that challenge. The Bunntyco–Cloudy Clime team had moved their horses in. Tim Leonard, captain, was still suiting up. Harold Barry was over at the edge of the field, the rest of that team, the Tulsa-Greenhill group were dressing, and waiting and watching. They were a 20 goal squad. Bunntyco–Cloudy Clime was rated at 22.

Hap Sharp was strapping on a pair of knee protectors; he's the Hap Sharp of the Chapparrell racing group and right now, he was the captain of the Tulsa team. Dr. Billy Linfoot came over to talk with him. Linfoot would be watching critically. He was Oakbrook's nine-goaler and he'd

be riding against the winners of this match for the full championship, later. Linfoot is a California veterinarian, and another of the pro players. He's little, light and balding and looks a bit like a former film history professor of mine. Linfoot had followed the rodeo circuit during his Colorado college days, then moved solidly into polo. When I met him at the Open he was working on a polo book which, among other things, would offer a mathematical formula for prejudging a team's success. You could definitely say he was a student of the sport.

But by now it was three, and the teams, mounted, moved to the ends of the field and started the slow, solemn procession toward the center where they'd flip a coin to choose their goals.

And the spectators, and there weren't very many, watched as they might have watched the start of a joust.

It is a curious thing about me and polo. But,

while I can watch a game and carefully follow the action, I find myself seeing it as its parts and not the whole. Polo becomes, for me, the colored shirts, the white breeches, the tall boots, the chestnut horses, the fast tug of a hand on a rein, the sun lighting up a horseshoe as the pony rides away from you, it's the wood on wood clack of stick on ball, and the strangely slow movement of fast action seen from a long way off, it's the red flag flapping up behind the goal posts as a verification of a score, and it's the hard breath and foamy sweat on the horses after they've played their 7 1/2-minute period and can stand resting.

The grooms grab the horses from the players and hold the fresh horses ready for mounting, and the game goes on as a new period starts. The hooves kick up pieces of turf and the riders move toward the ball, standing slightly in their stirrups, leaning in and getting a full body swing, pushing the ball off in the direction they want it to go. They pass it, and play it down and maybe score, or maybe watch it get taken away, and regroup for defense. But they play it the way Harold Barry would want it played—"well, you know, the best defense is still a good offense"—and at halfway through the score is Tulsa 4 and Bunntyco 2. The rest is longer now. I shoot some stuff along the sidelines and stop for a cigarette. The spectators. I watch them. They're almost like a club themselves. That's something worth noting. "Polo fans are different," Barry told me, "They'll come to watch polo and turn down all other sports to do it."

But there really aren't that many.

Polo moved into Argentina in the twentieth century, and it's become something of a national sport there. Joe Barry is a young player with experience and a six-goal rating. They tell you about his long shots, and how accurate he is. And he'll tell you about going down to Argentina to play. There were about 30,000 spectators watching his first Argentinean game.

What did you think when you went out and saw that many people?

"I thought, man what have I been missing all this time? And you know, they knew what was going on, too. There wasn't any public address system. . . . They'd yell for all the good plays, even the ones we made, and they knew if there

was a bad call or if the umpires had missed a foul, and they'd let you know that, too."

Then it was time again, and the Barrys and Hap Sharp and Rube Evans rode back out and started the rout of the Bunntyco team.

After the match had ended, the Tulsa-Greenhill group dismounted and walked to the table where they got their silver bowl trophies and drank champagne, in the tradition of victors, from the passed loving cup.

They looked happy, and rather pleased.

And then they walked away.

7

POWERBOAT

Flat—that's how they want it. Flat as a layed out mirror. Flat and level and damned near as solid as muddy glass. Flat and smooth, and probably just about as damp as wet concrete. That's what they look for. And this is where they found it, or almost, or good enough. If not perfect, if it gets choppy—not choppy like a sailor with a sail boat would say choppy, but kind of ruffled around the edges—then it gets more dangerous, speed drops, and the boats just don't run up to capacity. Now if you want to see what they were looking for, and what they found, just bend your car around some of those macadam backroads in the Illinois countryside until you've twisted through the right trees and followed the right signs and found—even before you've gotten properly into town—that you can hear a buzzing, sawing, high sort of sound. It's engines, you know that by now, and it's racing engines, and you know that, too, and the sound is coming from the other side of the little city. It's coming from over there.

There is Lake DePue. The town is DePue, Illinois, and named—no doubt—for the lake. The lake that touches it, that once was the other-side of main street, that Father Marquette himself found back in 1673 or so when he and his men missed the Illinois River. But Marquette found more than that lake. He found the citizens of the area. They came out to meet the Jesuit and his fellow-explorers. After a little conversation, the Indians gave these white fellows heaps of corn and buffalo meat to help them back along their way. And, when the canoes were ready to dip back into the water and head out toward the river, out toward sights strange to those who have not seen them, the Indians decorated those French canoes with flowers—good luck, peace or almost anything else you want to make out of it.

Marquette is gone, of course, and so are the Indians. Some corn remains, but you don't run across many buffalo. Now what about the canoes? Well, some still float by, but you're more apt to see motor-powered boats running up the lake. And if you catch the right weekend—which was the last day of July and the first two of August this 1970—the canoes are gone and replaced by hydroplanes and runabouts. Skimpy bottomed, skim-the-water, around-a-course and not-any-good-for-any-thing-but-racing boats.

Racing is what it's all about. That's why they've come from New York, Iowa, California, Texas and a lot of other places. That's why they've brought their boats. And that is definitely why I am here watching them.

These are the alky-burners. Powered by strange, and not so strange, fuel mixtures, they can be worked over and bred into racing form in somebody's backyard. They aren't the stocks. They aren't the big haruuummmmmphing ocean racing inboards either—powered by automotive engines and lashing back at the sea. They are no more than they pretend to be, the top of what little

outboards can run. Racers clamp motors onto the backs of their boats—these runabouts and hydroplanes. And they clamp their boats onto their trailers and their trailers onto their cars, and probably themselves at their car's wheel and drive for here. This is one of the big ones. It's the American Power Boat Association (APBA) National races. Later in the year the other big race sanctioning organization, the National Outboard Association (NOA), will have their show in Louisiana. Before these two, there will be a few, maybe three, big races that can draw contestants from the edges of the continent. And then the season is over. It ends as quietly as it starts, and a whole lot of people never even knew it happened.

Trials now on that flat-muddy-dirty-green-brown water, and the boats which are out send screams of spray flipping back from their butts, and tipping along on the edge of the water—they scream and smoke and spew. All along the bank, the northern edge, that is, the trailers and boats and mechanic-driver-friends-watchers in straw hats and striped short-sleeved shirts and Levis or wading boots or wet cotton trousers are extending the lake back, being, in a way, a reverse flood that comes this time of year. Back along that line, back up that bank and down, down to the West so it's under some tree-shade, is a hard-driven stationwagon and a line of people.

There are two free-floaters in this line. They've got on name tags and they're from a sparkplug company. One is standing beside the line and walking down, handing out pieces of paper and having people sign them.

"This is your publicity release. It gives us the right to use you in our advertising if you win."

That's how they pay for their sparkplugs. Slip of paper, sign, be handed a decal with the right logos and release that paper and latch onto the boxes of new plugs, lifted out of the cardboard boxes that sag the station wagon.

The other free-floater isn't floating, but he isn't in the line. He's by the tailgate of the station wagon, handing out the plugs. He's got white-gray hair that's in a ruffled short cut so it looks like some sort of frozen tundra weed and he's got this lined, weather soaked face that seems just right for the hair.

I stand there for a little while, looking over

this operation and keeping in the shade, and trying to catch a little of what breeze there is. Now I enjoy the heat, and I miss the sun every minute it's gone, but I figure I might as well take it a little easy, and catch this scene because my hat brim is probably so wet you could ring it out and I'm not being baked—which I would enjoy too much—but am being steamed, slowly, in the muggy Eastern-Midwestern air.

The racers in line don't look too concerned about the weather. They don't even look like they are thinking about it. The Champion man is checking the thermometer every so often and saying things about—must be where we got it. Surely it's not that far over a hundred.

Before, there were more faces, more hands, no

"Oh. Well, I'd say for the most part, they've just grown older."

"What do you mean?"

"Same faces. Same people. Just older."

"Not many new people, kids, getting into it here, huh?"

"Not really. It's too expensive for them. Now the stocks are a little different. But here, it's pretty much the same crowd."

Down, along the bank, up through on the east edge of the pits (they've got to call them something) it's gumbo ooze and sucking along at your boots as you walk down to where the little crowd is standing. White hair fluffed by the wind, steel-gray-white caught and held under a Western-styled straw that is so rough worn it just barely still looks like a hat, big, beefy men who've gotten weight from alcohol and buff brown faces from sun or water and look tough and capable and—business-like (which is not to say like businessmen). Hands

time for temperature readings.

"Good morning, Skip."

"Good morning," says Skip Mason, dipping his hands into the station wagon, "What do you need?"

And handing out boxes of 84s and 87s and the hand catches them and moves off into the southwest.

Skip has been handing out these sparkplug boxes for more than a decade.

"That's a long time. Not just with boats, right?"

"Oh, no, I make all sorts of different races, but I've been doing boats about that long."

"Well it's obvious that in that long boats have changed, and something of the racing styles have had to change. But. But what about the people?"

"Humm?"

"What about the racers? Are they different now than they were when you started? Different kinds of people, you understand?"

are stout, with fingers thick and solid. Not like looking at hands where the fingers draw in above the middle knuckle and light leaks through the flattened palm and you can say, well you can see he never did any work. No not like that. Not like that at all.

The washed-out olive wading boots on the feet and legs of Homer Kincaid seem to be seeping water. But that needn't be uncomfortable. The water is not cold. He is stalking, now, or seems to be stalking, walking out and around the boat that is laid out like a door, resting on the special holders that are properly padded but look a lot like sawhorses. Kincaid wades up on his motor, and is twisting and turning and seeing things.

Things?

Things. Because to Homer Kincaid and all of the other owner-driver-mechanics all along the edge of this lake, those motors are not motors. They have long ago become much more than that. They are very special racing engines—they are the

racing engines which Homer or Lee or Jim or Jerry have been working on since before they got here. They are moving, vibrating instruments with a lot of a person bound up in them. They have a sound like all of the other sounds, yet— different. And that is true here and that was true with the karters and the bikers and all of the others who have sweated in the name of pleasure over some moving hunk of metal.

Flash back to the night before this day. The sun has finally gone down, the night air has swept a hint of coolness from the lake and suggested it on shore. I'm sitting on a green park bench high up on the bank above the lake. The arc lights have come on and the mosquitoes are singing and seeking and finding. Back, behind where I sit, the night is more now. Yellow lights cast curious shadows over the people. All the people. Many people in the park, piled up against each other in the tightly crowded pavillion where all through the day the cooking and feeding goes on, which is the source of revenue to the town, the reason why there is no charge for coming and watching the sport. A band, itinerant rock group with name-painted-on-their-vehicle vehicle, is swaying and moving the music out and around the people like a little pinball ball bouncing off its objects and then the music escapes into the night.

"At ten o'clock," someone says, in an official voice, "everybody is supposed to be out of the pits. At ten o'clock the pits will be closed. Everybody is supposed to be out of the pits by ten o'clock." Then, in an afterthought manner but

And he's making his moves sharper still. But he loses this race.

"The pit area is closed.

"The pit area is closed.

"Will all boaters please leave the pit area immediately?"

Just a voice. Just night. Just dark with a little white from those high-up artificial sun arc lamps.

He's walking away now, at an angle from me, moving away. He's turning, still moving in a slow way, but looking back as a hitchhiker looks back up the road he's walking. Then he rubs his hair

still the same official, public-address-system megaphoned voice: "The pits will be opened again at seven o'clock tomorrow morning."

And he's almost alone down there anyway. And soon he is alone. And the feeling moves up from down below the bank, down by the edge of the water, down in the half-light of arc-bright and dark shadow, down from his boat—get it done, hurry to get it done, really into it. The moves, all of them.

back with one hand and pauses, holding that look, that look back. Then he turns and walks up the bank and disappears into the dark.

"Rolling, rolling, rolling on the river." The lyric that's escaped from the pavillion.

Ten minutes later. Back down the bank. Same figure? Yes. Same figure. But with a paper carton in his hand, he pauses, rips it open and slips the big beige plastic sacks out of it. Utility bags, Hefty bags, beige and folded. He shakes one open and

then, very gently, very carefully, he moves around the engine, pulling the bag down onto it, tucking a little here, tugging a little there. Carefully arranging the bag as a cover for the engine. Done. Then he turns and walks straight off and up the bank and into the night.

Kincaid has stopped stalking, and is standing on the muddy bank looking down the line and saying there's really somebody I should meet. Somebody named Dub Parker, and pretty soon here comes Dub Parker and he walks up and Kincaid tells me here's someone I should meet. This skinny man with grease on his hands and years on his head.

And soon they get to talking with me mostly listening.

"Used to run four heats in a day," says Kincaid, "and maybe win one and place second in the other."

"Why, we've went hungry to race, and bought groceries later," says Parker.

And they talk about another race and Dub invites Kincaid down to stay at his place and "we can pull your engine in and work on it, too."

So they talk about motors.

"No two of those motors will run identical," Parker tells me. And then they slip back into what fun it had been and Parker remembers, "I got a double hernia playing football and didn't even have enough money for the operation." It was all always for the racing. And how they'd drive away to see a race with the racers they knew about and would sleep in the car and then drive right on straight back, being hungry and thinking about how good any old dry sandwich might be just then. And how when they'd get enough money to get a boat and engine it was only good for a little while. You'd get one that wasn't quite up to the others and stay in last place for four years, but—by God—that'd teach you something about racing and then you'd decide that the only way, the only, only way to get ahead or even stay even was to start building and doing your own work. So Parker got this incredible engine that he won about 78 first places with, without a loss.

And, well, it's kind of like somebody else said about the whole thing: "Before you get to be a good winner, you've got to be a good loser." And

what's really strange is that he believed that. Yeah. Now that's all right.

"The competition is keen," Kincaid is saying to me, "but it's clean. They're clean sportsmen here. And they'll help each other out."

Now he's stalking his motor again.

"The biggest thing to do is work on your motor. Just to get it running. Most of these drivers are pretty good mechanics. And," he looks back up,

"you've got to be an expert, almost, in about ten fields to keep one of these things going."

All Billy Seebold has to do is keep one going once it's gotten into the water. That's all. All? Well, Seebold is a driver and about as close to a pro driver as you're going to find here. Now Homer and Dub and the rest get paid if they win, or place well enough, but it's like nothing money and if they were operating under amateur rules which allowed for some transportation money they

might just make more. And Homer and Dub and the others work their motors over, work their boats over and put the two together, climb on and rev off to spin with the second hand and hit the flying start fast and race.

Billy Seebold, he just stands there.

Marshall Grant has the boats that Billy drives.

"So she finally comes up," Grant is talking, "and she says to me, 'Well, I've been watching and it looks to me like this Billy Seebold doesn't do anything but drive!' And I said, 'Lady, if he does it right, that's enough.'"

And later to me, "If he don't win, I don't feel it's his fault."

For Grant, the fun comes from working the boats into condition to hit that water. Square-big and blond headed, his words come out with a Southern accent, and—as Johnny Cash's bass guitar player (16 years—so far—with Cash, "I'm part of Johnny and he's part of me.")—he has the time and money to pursue his sport. And he pursues it in style.

The pit area is crowded with his boats, white with red flares of paint and names like "Miss Folsom" and "Ring of Fire I" and "Ring of Fire

114

II" and even "A Boat Named Sue." The Big K–4 is bold on the boats and they're all clean, as clean, no cleaner than the whole pit area—which is plenty clean.

And there's Seebold, knit pull-over, Levis, big orange life preserver getting worn like a gambler's vest. Seebold is from St. Louis. Looking handsome

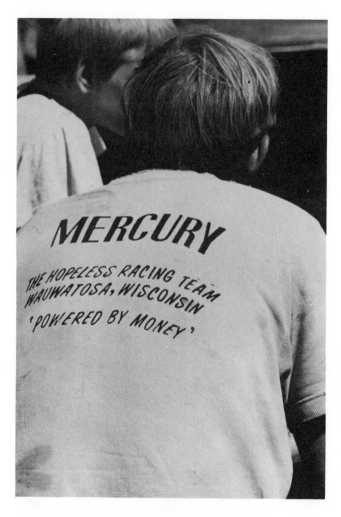

and clean-cut-rugged just the way you'd figure a race-boat jockey should. But being quiet and not walking cocky. Sure, but not cocky.

And. Is there any strategy in this kind of racing? How do you play it?

"Start first," he says, "and improve your position."

Like it's been rehearsed.

Well, why not?

And anyway, starting first isn't all that easy.

Off shore sits a barge. And on that barge are judges, and stopwatches and a massive big clock

and a cannon. And they've all got something to do with how you start.

The clock is an electrical-mechanical monster that should fire, automatically, that cannon five minutes before the start of the race. The metallic-voiced announcer will probably say, "Five minutes, that was the five minute signal." He's been triggered by the gun that was triggered by the clock.

And it's time for the racers to shoot off into the flat, vaguely rippling waters. For the next four minutes the boats can leave the pits and move out onto the course, building up speed, handling and fighting to stretch the time tight, tighter than a slingshot, and rocket across the starting line just as the signal goes. After the one-minute gun the big clock takes over. Six feet high and wide. The big clock. A clock face as tall as a man and with this disc instead of hands, this black disc that starts eating up pieces of the clock, covering it second by second. From sixty seconds to start it moves its way around. The boaters must be out, must be moving, must be twisting and turning through before-the-fact paces that will put them in a prime position. Then, close, close now, the disc is nibbling away, and the boats are into the straight run right for the line by the barge, by the clock, by the cannon. Right down there. The seconds moving off, no way to know it but to feel it and they're fast up on it and then—BAM: cannon crackles with one blank blast and it's started. And it's close. It's almost always very close. Judges are leaning with their noses pointed at that starting line, that magical point. Judges are craning their necks, keeping their ear ready for the first fraction of a cannon shell explosion. How does it come together? Anyone across the line before the gun goes is disqualified—if it's called. So races aren't finished until the judges have named the legal finishers.

"Start first and improve your position."

But it's not all that easy, right?

"That's where your races are won or lost all right—right there on the starting line."

And more than one has said something like that.

If Wayne Baldwin hasn't said it yet he probably will before it's all over. Give him time. Right now he's only 21. His dripping moustache and long (or what passes for long) hair looks out of place at this time with most segments of this crowd which he has fallen into. And he fell, no question about that. This Texan was thinking about boat racing, I'm not clear why, and decided he'd take it up. He did. The first race he ever saw was also the first one he ever ran.

"I didn't really know what I was doing. I just got out and went round and round."

And around his neck, he's got a St. Jude medal. Jude, as you probably know, is patron of hopeless tasks.

"Does it work?"

"Not yet."

Mark Baldwin, brother to Wayne, is younger and blonder haired and came along for the ride and stayed to be pit crew. And it's all great getting-into-late-summer fun.

Lee St. Claire, at this time, is 61. He's just cut back on his racing "going strictly runabout now" and looking back just a bit.

"It's quite a hobby. I've been all over the country. But it's just a hobby, like your golf and hunting.

"But I've got every trophy in the book except the world trophy."

And then he's talking about an old engine—a 22 Evinrude that was strapped onto a pleasure boat and how a few guys would race each other on a Sunday afternoon—"a race of our own." It went 37 miles per hour. "I worked it up to about 70 or 90. The same cubic inches and same type of engine—the C-Service."

I walked back to talk to Grant. He was sitting in a little shade, his plantation straw's brim was down all around and he was just waiting.

"You've got to have a love for the sport . . . and work hard as hell. And you can be a winner way over your percent and still be losing money." He squints up toward the sun and checks his watch.

"And you've got to accept the fact that you are going to lose. Take this. You're racing against the entire membership of this association. It's just plain hard to win."

They were all going to have their chance because the qualifying heats—the races to be able to race—were over and the races begun, the real for-the-national-championship races. Jerry Peterson is one who didn't qualify. At 23 he's one of the new ones, and at this time a Des Moines boat dealer is backing his play. His best shot was at the F Hydro title—the heaviest class. He won that in the NOA meets last year. But suddenly he's dead in the water—his engine was still screaming but dead. Later, on the bank, he showed me the sheered off propeller. The torque had twisted it apart.

And only an hour earlier he'd said:

"Come on in. I've got to gap a couple of plugs." And I'd walked into the littered work area and asked about him and found out he was 23 and had raced for 10 of those years.

"You were supposed to have been 16, but I was big for my age. They never really asked and I never really said." So, how does it start so soon? "Dad and I were always interested in boats. We went to a race and bought some junk and just

started racing." And keep it up? "It's a real thrill racing on the water—going at high speed. It's not like on the ground. I like motorcycles, but you don't get the same thrill." How about the other racers? "The drivers have a real friendly attitude toward each other. It's not cut throat. They'll help a guy out, lend their parts. The people are just fabulous."

Now, on the bank with a white shirt, dry and fresh and loose on his bony body, he walks east, stops and holds out the prop that's small and pinwheel-like and just sheered the hell off.

"Too much torque."

"That really went."

"Yeah."

"Well. Where are you headed?"

"Oh. I've got to take this back."

"Back?"

"Yeah, I borrowed it from a guy."

And on down the edge of the lake, walking and trying to smile and seeming positive even if it's over. And what was it the man said—to be a good winner, you got to be a good loser first? And every so often we all need a lesson in luck.

And now Grant, who has been spending a lot of time in the pits working over his engines, a

lot more time than he would like to have spent, is starting to say things like:

"I got in it gradually. I started out with an A and just kept climbing the ladder. Now I've got everything but an A." And looking at the boats, "Maybe we should get an A and get rid of everything else."

Then it's come down to it. And the cannon sounds and the red flag runs up and it's A racing

runabouts out and onto the lake. Runabouts, knife-nosed, tipping, slicing boats, raising up and cutting along. And the races go on with the boats in classes from A to F, hydroplanes, which skim along on the edge where water and air meet, and runabouts. The top for this course is an F-hydro-held 110 miles per hour. But in 1970 more weight is required. That made riding safer, kept those boats from being powered into loops and, in effect, made

the smaller engined D class a little faster—not faster than the record but faster than the F's—because their weight was still down.

The odd class is C-Service. These motors date from the days of alcohol prohibition and are very nearly the first of the real outboard motors. Some time ago the decision was made to keep them racing. It's a slow show but the well-worked-over engines keep a piece of the sport's history right there on the course.

But now, watch the boats race. Hydroplanes rounding the course, it's marked by buoys and has only left turns, which are like controlled slides dirt track drivers slip their cars through. The first boat goes a bit wide and the next one bolts through right near the marker then cuts into his slide and slips out in front of number one. He's got the lead and moves down into the straight, the straight clear across the course, the spray, in its rooster-tail, shooting up behind, the boat lifting and gliding and dancing there on the rippled water, churning out a hole, chopping it up, kicking it back and moving into the next turn. And again and again and again. Now one is out, haze and smoke and spray hide him. But there—there now —his hands are in the air over his flame-colored helmet, high and he's all right. All he can do is wait and watch and take the tow rope when it comes dragging by.

Up along the bank the racers are watching, those not still working over engines, or dressing, or just worrying too hard. Others are up on top of trailers and roof areas, with field glasses turned on the course, scanning the field, seeing the spray popping back and laying down like heavy smoke.

And by now, someone is probably in the lead, in there to stay, unless he stops running. But that's part of the game, too. Listen—the engine over there sounds rough, buzzing and burring and sounding altogether bad and the people by the bank are wading out a bit and watching the last of the laps. Racers for the next round are getting their boats floating. Some people way up the hill tip bourbon from a half-pint into Coca-Cola cups, a six year old asks his mother for a drink of water. A contestant's friend is saying—"Well damn it all anyhow" and the first boat is taking the finish flag.

And when the finish flags have all finished flapping, Bob Wannamaker, the referee, can say,

"There have been over 2,000 boats go through the first turn without the ambulance whining away once."

Then Al with the fluffy, white hair, can catch you and say, "Some of them you take first. Some of them you take last. Some days the motor is just right, some days it's all wrong. Just like you. Some days you feel good, and some days you don't."

Then check the records a bit. No one really hurt here. Last year eleven went to the hospital on the last day. This year speeds were down. That was a combination of the extra weight and the crosswind. There was a record crowd of spectators, 467 boats (the 2,000 approximated the number of times boats went into that first turn) and there were new national winners.

Then he comes. The voice that has it all. The boat-racer moves up, gives you that shrug-smile combination and says,

"Why would a guy spend two thousand dollars and travel two thousand miles to win 120 bucks?

"It don't make sense."

Then he lets the shrug go and keeps the smile and—yeah—it makes sense.

I know, for an instance, that, if you want to play this way, you can make the river stand for all sorts of other things. But doing that it seems to me is taking your eye off the ball; making it more than what it is lessens it. Just to see it clear is plenty.—Ken Kesey

8
WILD WATER

It is a sound.

It is a sound like no other sound. It is a sound like no other sound I have ever heard. It is a sound like no other sound I have ever heard, I think. It is a sound I wake up hearing and thinking railroad cars are switching just beyond the window. But there are no railroad trains there now, only the tracks. Tracks alone and empty and just there waiting and standing, or laying, in front of a hill which drops sharply to it, to the sound and more than the sound—to the river.

It is a sound.

It is the sound. It is the sound of the river, the river rushing, the river of white water moving down out of the hills, fast (not fast you understand, but fast all the same). It is the sound the river makes and when you have heard it you remember it. And then it is just there and it lays there, like the river, forgotten until something leaves your brain and the sound creeps back up and becomes noticed and you wonder how you were able to not hear it. But you are. And the sound will be there but your attention will not be until that happens again and the sound comes back and the sound is more than there. The sound is a sound that calls you down, down to the edge of the river, or close to the edge, to the higher ground that stays there so you stare down into the water which is moving along, gray and green and brown and—white—white around the rocks, white, shattering over them, white swirling, white and hard and wild.

It is a sound.

It is a call.

And men from around the world have come here to answer it.

Now if you are in this country, this area, this thing called the United States of America, and have spent your times in the plains then you know that when you move east for the first time after a long time of not moving east you slice off pieces of history. You do not feel this as you motor past the cities. You feel this as you motor past the rivers. The Missouri yields to the Ohio, the Ohio yields to the Mississippi, the Mississippi to the Wabash, the Wabash to the Allegheny—now do you feel it?—the Allegheny to the Potomac—and now, now, now do you ever feel it?—and the Potomac yields to the Delaware and just to history itself. There is a sense, not of tameness, but of age and with the quiet of age and the distance of time when such an age was youth.

Now go west and feel it, raw and biting with rivers with names that make magic and move on and cross the Rio Grande, the Pecos, the Cimmaron, the Red, the Snake, the Colorado, the

Feather, the Kern. And they are open and waiting and western. And frozen into time. Changing but keeping what they had in your mind.

From Leadville down it flows. Down the mountains and dropping and rushing and growing and streaming and dropping and plowing through the plains. From Turquoise Lake beneath the Sanatch Range it goes down, down, drawing off the waters of the Cottonwood Creek, of the Grape Creek, Hardscrabble Creek, High Creek, Timpas Creek, Rule Creek, Clay Creek and the Purgatory River. Drawing off those waters, and more, and moving on and on across the plains.

Down the mountains, beneath Turquoise Lake, lower than Leadville, Granite and Buena Vista, the river goes rushing, sounding its sound. Under the bridges of the Rio Grande and Western Railroad. Down and below the bridge of the town. What town? Salida town. Down goes the Arkansas. Yes, Down.

Late afternoon, warm and nice and sun being bright and kind, I cross the bridge of that town over that river, and pause to look down, and watch it move past the railroad trestle, watch it yield to the blades holding up that bridge and moving on to be itself—one river—just past them. The river is dark, and has a layer of dirt over it, and the green—see that—the green stripe running through it.

The stripe runs down, under the bridge. I walk along the line of cars that are parked up next to the wall of the bridge and go on across it in all of its shortness, from the side with the bus and railroad terminal to the side with the boathouse and the town. The boathouse. The boathouse door stands open, and just off the bridge, nothing between the boathouse building and the river except for the drop of the land. The boathouse, an old hotel, a leftover from a time when Salida was a Colorado town and not just a town in Colorado. Someone is just standing there. He looks only a little older than me. And he is looking at the river.

From Canada he came, down the long way south, with his wife he came, bringing a Dalmation dog, a big pickup truck and a camper on its back, a towed, mobile boat rack, and boats. Boats of fiberglass and paddles of wood. Kayak boats, but like no Eskimo ever made. In colors that would sparkle on the river. Light, knife-nosed, tough little boats. And he who brought them is standing, staring at the river.

Keith Daniel is staring at the river.

Keith Daniel is a good place to start.

His voice carries a trace of Western Canada and his face is sharp and set, not formed by many years, but set so you can see how it will form. He is neither big nor small. Now he is smiling and happy and it is good to be here and knowing you can run this river on different days and run it for a prize. It is good, too, to find someone else you hadn't known and someone who has come from a distance to learn about this sport which is so much of your life.

So he talks and tells a hundred things about this running of rivers, this boating and one man, himself, who plays this game with himself and with the river.

The Slalom? How do you figure that one? The downriver race describes itself, so I'll tell you about the slalom in case you don't know how that works. The boats are set off separately and go for the gates—and there are gates, two poles hung parallel and those are your markers, it's the poles that the boat and man must go through—clear, not touching, not touching even with a paddle. The gates are set up differently: some are straight, go through pointing right down river, some are reverse gates that you'd have to clear backwards, some are up-river and you'd have to paddle into the current to get through them. Others can be

set wide horizontally to each other but one not that much in front of the other so you'd be moving across the stream, bucking the river to hold your own. If you miss a gate you lose 100 points. If you hit it from the outside or don't follow directions properly you lose 50. If you touch a pole from the inside you lose 10, two touches or touching both poles and it's 20. The total penalty points are added directly to the amount of time, in seconds, it takes you to get from the start to the finish of the course. And that total is your score. Obviously the lowest score wins. And that is not what a slalom is, but, quickly, how it is scored.

How it works is different. And that can wait for a different time in telling.

Daniel and I walked inside to look at the boats. Oh yes, they look like boats, but not so much like boats that you wouldn't notice at once that they are special and say: what do you suppose they use them things for?

Stacked in what once must have been the wooden-floored lobby of this place when it was a hotel and tobacco and cigars were sold and newspapers dropped off from the traveling through trains and a high-topped desk held up a black-bound register, stacked all across that flooring were boats. The kayak is straighter, its cockpit opening is higher than its ends. The rider fits himself through the hole and sits with legs thrust out in front of him. With the canoes, the ends curve back up to be as high as that cockpit opening; the paddler kneels. With a kayak the paddles are one long pole with the blades on both ends, the canoe paddle is one blade and you paddle from one side of it. They call the canoes Canadian racing canoes and they are different from the other canoes you may have seen. They reach up and cover themselves just like the kayaks, and a waterproof spray-shield stretches across the ridge of the cockpit opening and draws tight against the waist of its paddler. There are two-person canoes, too. And there are different types of kayaks. The slalom boat is slower but steadier and looks a bit blunter. The downriver type is faster, but tippier. It is built for the speed —the stability will just have to take care of itself.

These boats are lying, now, on the floor of this building. They are fiberglass and of various colors, but that is not what you will notice. They are there, simply there, and looking as if they are at rest in this dark, splotched lighting.

To the side, and below them, the river is not at rest.

The next morning in what I would call cold, which perhaps isn't, Tom Johnson was looking at the river. Short and built heavy the way you might like to think bare-knuckle boxers used to be built, Johnson is the old man in the game. This June, this 1970, this race he is 52. He had been up early in this cold and into that river and sampling it. Now he was interested in finding some products at the shipping office. If they came, he was going to build a boat.

"Well," he says, "I've been interested in canoes all my life. When I was 19 I built my first one. And in 1942 I built the first fiberglass canoe."

He amends that, and says he certainly thinks it was the first and has not yet found anyone who built one before that—and he's been looking.

"I ran my first white water race in 1962. I bought a boat and began to learn in an area where nobody had boats," he was in Los Angeles. "So I started a club. You see if you don't have somebody to do your sport, to participate with, it's not really as interesting."

You see. Johnson is a competitor. And he takes his play seriously. He had been a fireman in Los Angeles but was retired young—a victim of a tough trade. One pectoral muscle was pretty much ruined. It is not hard where yours is hard, and his paddling, especially for kayak, has a singular style about it, a higher arc which moves a lot of the work onto the back muscles. And that is apt to make one tired.

The pectoral, or if you prefer the pectoralis major, does a lot of work—it flexes and adducts

the arm, elevates the shoulder and draws it forward and makes the forward and medial traction motion of the arm and shoulder. In short, you should need it to paddle.

Johnson is operating, essentially, without one of these muscles. And operating well. "We just kind of get to a point where people expect a guy 50 years old has had it," he says. "And the guy just goes along with the bunch. Well I don't think it has to be that way. It's quite possible I can be right up there, in the slalom. That's something that requires a certain amount of skill."

Downriver racing?

"Well it's tough for anybody to get themselves into a condition to go for full tilt for two hours."

The fiberglass resins aren't at the freight depot yet. So we walk along by the river for a few more minutes.

"You see how speed is relative," he asks me.

"What do you mean?"

"That river. Now it sounds big, so maybe you think it's fast."

"Yeah, I guess I'd call it fast."

"But it's probably only going about four miles an hour past here."

"That doesn't sound fast."

"Well, speed kills. And for water that might be fast enough. The danger is that we're not amphibious. We're out of our element. In the water if you capsize and can't manage to make it ashore," he shrugs, "you've had it."

He squats down, getting closer to the river.

"The bad places," he says, "are where there are obstructions—bridges."

He's looking at me more than at the river, now.

"These things, these boats started out as utility boats. . . . Indians, they could stuff it under a bush and go on. Sooner or later they're going to start some sort of competition."

"How come you compete? Why do you do it?"

"The answer to that is like when they ask why does the guy climb a mountain. You know it's possible. You see other guys doing it. Somebody says it's impossible. Well, I think I can figure a way to make it possible. And when you do you're going through a river that was unnavigable any other way."

Eventually the mountains yield the sun to the sky and the day grows in warmth. Then people come out of the boathouse, they come out at staggered intervals. Daniel comes out and walks with the tall Dalmatian down to the river. As the day's colors come up fuller, others come out and some cross from the boathouse to the park that lies across the street. Soon a small, portable carnival will be set up at one end of it—the end away from the river. There is a looking at the sky, now, and a looking at the river. The sky is clear and the river is fuller.

Later there will be a time for practice, and a time to draw for the numbers.

This whole event has a way of progressing in stages, a little at a time. Each one seeming important. Each one leading a little closer to Sunday, a little closer to more than 25 miles of downriver race. And people keep coming out of the boathouse. Bernt Kast comes out of the boathouse. He is walking like he knows he is going to win. He is 21, from West Germany, with long hair and a wide smile. He has a gymnast's build, broad through shoulders and back, narrowing. I don't remember if he had on that particular shirt on that particular day, but it does not matter. Even without that printed reminder, he was—at this time—the champion racer of the world. Other racers may have suggested that someone else could win, but had it come down to betting, their money would have ridden on Kast.

He started when he was 14 and just kept it up. He joined a club in Nuremburg. "First you want some paddling," he says, "and then . . . well, it's always the same."

"Yes," says Daniel who's standing with us, "the challenge is there."

And well now, if that doesn't sound just all together too right. Check this. It's February 1949, and a couple of businessmen are spending their time sipping coffee. Well, one thing and another and one says I'll race you down that Arkansas River, from here to Canyon City. And, yeah, drinking coffee in February it's all right to take that on and so it's set. Well, of course, the word gets around and some people show up taking this idea seriously. It's something of a surprise when a couple of young Swiss men saunter into town and say they've been running rivers in the country and heard about the race and where the hell do they sign up. So.

So. Fifty-six miles from Salida down the Arkansas through the Royal Gorge to Canyon City.

So. If it floats and you think you've got the guts you pick up something and get set to give it a try. And the Swiss gents unfold their boat and are really ready.

They're even serious.

And twenty-one other people must have been something, because they all entered. Somebody even thought the way to go was in the stripped off belly tank of an old bomber.

Yeah. Fifty-six miles.

And seven hours, eighteen minutes and thirteen seconds later, those two Swiss, Robert Ris and Max Romer, came out alive and winning and the only ones to finish.

Now. Do I have to tell you who didn't even run? Two very dry businessmen had started something more than they had ever expected.

The winners, after they'd dried off a bit, suggested the course be shortened. Two years later it was—to the 25.7 miles it's been from then through this 1970 running.

Peter Egger was standing on that bridge when I met him, too. He is from Orange, in New South Wales in Australia. He's an electrical engineer and this is, sort of, a vacation.

"If we had rivers like this," he was staring out over it now, "they'd put six dams on it—bing, bing, bing."

Egger is young, too. And he's tall and almost all angles. This would be about his eighth year in racing and he would be the first Australian to come to this Arkansas River race. He took the sport up "as a diversion from Scouting, getting a bit tired of it you see." He's not getting tired of this.

"You're competing against nature. If you do what you want to, you're defeating nature. If you can challenge nature and do it—it's a thrilling thing, like climbing the face of a mountain.

"It's you against the water, not you against the competition or anything else. It's a clean sport that way. You're competing against someone only indirectly.

"If you do it, you're defeating what nature set up."

Gunter Hemmersbach was living in Detroit, he had settled there from Germany—or settled for a while at least. At 32 he had seen a lot of the sport on both continents.

"It's nicer here to paddle," he told me, "It's still fun here, it just doesn't get as serious as in Europe." Then he told me about a race in 1963 in a town about the size of Salida where two clubs raced each other. "There are good, rough rivers in the Alps." He liked that. "I had belonged to a swimming club, kayak guys were looking for members, they talked to us about it, I tried it out and I liked it so much I said, 'I don't swim anymore.'"

And here, with Gunter, is someone who doesn't think of only competition. "No. I see it also as a hobby. I enjoy it also, just going down a good river."

As we talked, the sun continued to warm. And it felt very comfortable there, this mid-June day, to have the sun come down and be warm and yet still a little soft and to help get out the long cold chill of winter. For him this race was on the order of a minor pilgrimage. This race is more famous in Europe than in the United States. Now that he is here, the chance to run it would be an almost foolish thing to refuse. This race is, put simply, shaping up as a lot of things for a lot of people.

But then races have a tendency to be just that.

In the boathouse, in the dark of coming in from out of the day, in the lobby of the once hotel, Tom Johnson is making a boat. At the near-center of that room a mold is stretched out and into it go the strips of fiberglass cloth. They look, among other things, like bandaging. Johnson and his wife and the Eggers are moving around in the boathouse and soon enough the cloth will look like more than cloth and will be a boat that Johnson will make for Egger. The moves are rapid, the polyethylene resin is poured from a paper cup over the glass cloth. It's spread over, painted over. The cloth turns from white to a mud brown-black. Blue squeegees spread it in. People move fast, bending over the molding. Boats are stacked against the wall. The door is open and a man with glasses and a white sailor's hat walks in. He looks around, asks some pointless questions and leaves. Rapidly, the resin is spread, Johnson is making his moves sharp, underlying the rush, to get it spread evenly to dry evenly.

Drying, easily, the boat is untended for a while now. It sets in the two pieces of molding that will be top and bottom. Somewhere Mrs. Johnson has found a big broom and is pushing it across the floor.

"I hate messy places."

"You probably get stuck with cleaning up as well as helping build the boats, huh?"

"I don't mind it," she says and handles the broom crisper so that in a few more quick swatches she is through. The sealing that will soon come up is a one-man operation, so she wonders if Tom—and the Eggers too—would like some lunch, and, a little later, moves off fast to fix it.

But right now Tom Johnson is cleaning resin off his hands.

"The tough part," he says, "is to get them laminated together from the inside."

He straightens up.

"Then the tears start to roll."

Soon the hull is propped on its side, hanging from the front by a wire and laying, on its back tip, on a high piece of step-ladder. A single, harsh-bright bulb is hanging by its cord and Johnson is poking his head into the cockpit opening, tacking pieces of the glass cloth into a seam position between the hulls. That's the hard part, that's reaching and fitting and trying to get it down and hoping it works because that's all that holds the two halves together.

You can look at the boats, and thump them and see how hard and firm they feel. But when you have seen them transformed from strips of cloth and evil-smelling liquid, you understand that they come from something more fragile than the river —something, perhaps, as fragile as life itself.

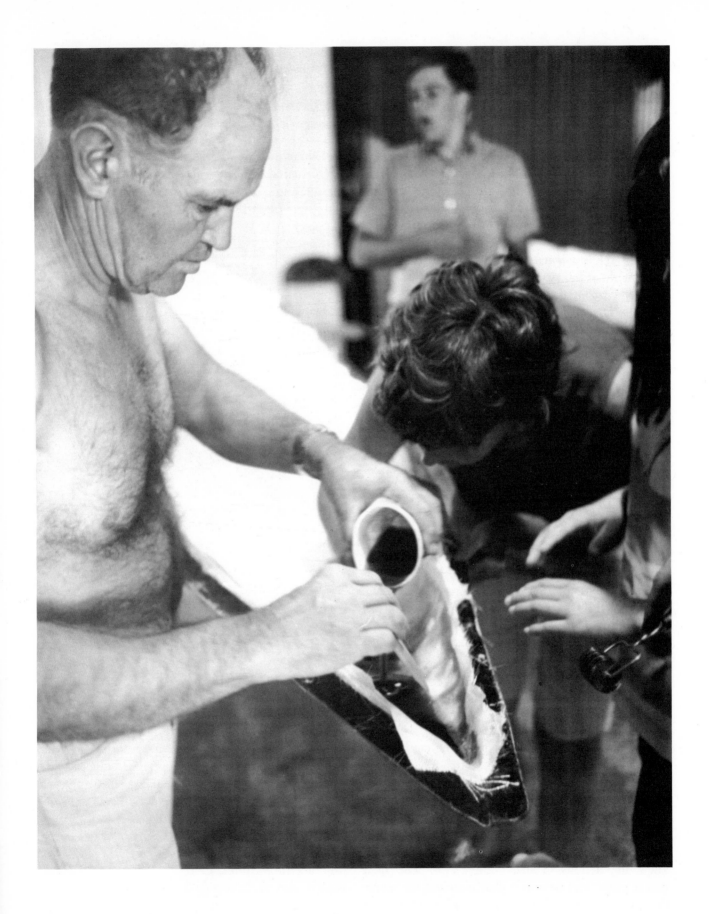

Stan and Ema Chladek were getting out of their car, the one with the Texas tags. He was a little afraid the police might ticket or tow it, but he wanted to leave it right in front of the boathouse for a few minutes. I told him there probably wouldn't be any problem, and if they ticketed it he could talk his way out of it. I believed that, I also wanted him to hold still long enough for me to ask him a few questions. He didn't get a ticket and he did talk.

While Ema watched the son closely, Stan Chladek stood on the sidewalk outside the boathouse. His bluejeans were new and cinched in tight with a heavy leather belt. They were not getting worn in the usual Western way. But then Chladek is from Czechoslovakia.

"Oh yes, the sport is more popular there than here, but not like motorcycle racing or that sort of thing, it's still a small sport. There are only amateurs. There are two very big races. And for one there may be 20,000 people.

"The paddlers specialize and they practice every-day. Of course not in the winter, but the season is from April through August.

"I don't know exactly why we like white water . . . slalom gates and white water . . . it is nice to race—to be first sometimes."

Chladek and his wife race, especially in the C2M class, the M means mixed, and the mixed means men and women. Most North Americans operate with the woman in front, working on steering, and the man in back, pushing. Europeans tend to reverse this.

"The first one is the engine of the boat," Chladek says. "If you have to drive the boat through the gate you need more power in the front. The downriver race, for me, too is similar."

This was a race he would run before leaving for Czechoslovakia. He had been teaching this year in Houston, and now had several weeks to see as much of the United States as he could cram in. And he and Ema were hungry for it. They had spent the afternoon driving through as many of the mountains as they could get to, and still get back in time to register for the races.

Watching them work out on the river you could see by the way they moved the boat that they knew the actions of each other well. The boat had a grace and flow to it that matched the water they ran in. The big orange boat bobbed and

bounced, but it appeared always to have a path it followed and the sway might have been set to a gentle bit of music.

It was dark, or almost dark, and the room was very crowded. The room was in the boathouse and the crowd were racers and officials and others. They had come in to draw for positions for the slalom and the downriver run. Positions have little but psychological value. The water does not get choppy because others have passed over it the way snow gets choppy from the skis of other racers.

Most of the paddlers, though, would prefer to start somewhere in the middle of the pack. The only meaning the numbers might have would be if you took what you drew in relation to what you wanted as an omen of how it would go. And to do that might be more than a little foolish.

Keith and Linda Daniel had told me to watch out for Roger Paris. They didn't know if he was coming to race, but they had heard he was coming. Paris has been a world champion, and he's won this race three times, in 1954, 1956 and 1958. He placed second in 1967. I checked up on him a little more. The address listed for him during

the three wins was Orleans, France. For the second-place year it was Carbondale, Colorado. There is a college there and he teaches French and coaches the kayak and ski teams. He is a certified ski instructor and mountain guide. There is more than a little coldness directed at him from some of the Salida officials, partly because of a question of his validity to race—essentially did he pay the entrance fee? The answer would never be as interesting as the question, and I suspect he enjoys the controversy and the reputation that comes with it as much as any man could.

I was not watching the door closely enough, but then I did not know who to watch for. Keith leaned over and said, "There he is." And I saw a man, short and thinly built, as brown as old leather, walking back in the room. His cut-off jeans were faded and short, and he was soon surrounded by his students.

It had been an excellent entrance.

I paid attention to the drawings, but I was really interested in them getting over so I could get a chance to talk to him.

The night was chilly on the F Street bridge. The sun was well down and the electric lights had come up to replace it. His followers, that's what I have to call them, stood close by him and listened.

It is his stage:

PARIS: Competition in every man . . . that's life. This is probably a substitute for what modern life does not give you. That's why people are climbing mountains. And you have to do it for yourself. We measure ourself against others . . . but first the race is against his own self and only then against others. With this sport it is always a question of speed and accuracy. And the two are antagonists.

Cut to black.

FADE IN: Morning in a valley in the Rockies. The sun is not yet over the mountains. I go downtown for coffee and several cigarettes. Boatracers haven't surfaced. They have time. They need what strength their sleep can give them. Walking across the F Street bridge I see that the water is even higher now.

Kast might just beat Hiebler's record. Some were starting to suggest that it might just get run in less than two hours.

Others disagreed.

And, anyway, now there is time to think about those slaloms. Each racer gets two runs, one on Friday, the next on Saturday. And the *Mountain Mail* carries a good weather notice—"Generally

A lot of flooding came in 1965. That year there had been plenty of snow in the mountains and it melted fast and forced the rivers full and flooded. That year Franz Hiebler, an Austrian paddler, had run to the Cotopaxi Bridge in two hours, three minutes and thirty-eight seconds. That was a record. The water has been lower since then. This year the water was rising. Racers would walk to the river in the morning, look at it and say it is up even more. Soon some were suggesting that

fair and warm through Sunday. Highest temperatures 90s southeast to 80s northwest 70s in the mountains. Low temperatures in the 50s at lower elevations 35 to 45 mountains"—and mentions Salida's high and low temperature that day: 80 and 35.

Keith, Linda and the Dalmation walk down to look at the course.

KEITH: It's going to take a 10 easy, probably a 50.

133

LINDA: Look at in front of gate four. Oh, that's got to be moved.

KEITH: That's no good. Have to see if we can get that moved. The only way to get that C–2 through is to come back through here.

LINDA: Well. After we get our practice run we'll know better.

KEITH (to me): It's a muscle course.

The water is up more and the pull is strong, a lot of the little eddies have been washed out, so there's no convenient way to put your boat with the current and hold. It all has to be done by hand. When the water is this fast, the upstream gates are simply there for the strong, the clean maneuvering and strategic approach are out. That's what it means when you call it a muscle course.

Johnson is even more disappointed.

Kast looks as unconcerned as usual.

Both Eggers are cautious.

And then the people come—bringing with them coolers and Coke, sunglasses and straw hats, binoculars and Boxer dogs, cameras, coats, best wishes and worst knowledge. They come. Together they have it all. There are those who have tried this river and those who do not know why it would be tried. There are those who watch the sport and those who suspect it is some roughneck stunt. They are all here, in short-sleeved shirts and half-held looks and sunshine.

Roger Paris is in the water. No shirt, no safety helmet, no life preserver. Roger Paris is scooting through the gates, testing them, trying them, performing through them. Roger Paris is showing how it should be done. There is no pressure, there, except as it comes from deep within where pressure is always the greatest. He is not racing and so is not limited to one runthrough with no stopping and doing a single gate a half dozen times until

you know it, no having to go against the competition when the watches are running and judges are sitting with their eyes upon the slalom poles. Roger Paris, looking tough and together with his boat, is in the water and, if we let him, teaching us all a little something.

Down go the questions, about gate three, or seven or whichever. Back come the answers that are stated so professionally in tone that they stand as a barricade against argument. If the questioner should have doubt, he would keep that doubt within.

The crowd is bigger.

picked up and relayed down. "Kast is next."

And there he goes—try and follow him, follow him with your eye. He is moving fast and sure and hitting it just the way you would want to, and he has the power—he is one of the possible beneficiaries of a muscle course slalom and no one will ever know if he needed it. But most would not believe he did.

Linda Daniel, her bobbed hair tucked under the louvered crash cap, is paddling hard, turning back into the current. Keith is by the bank. She's headed into the upstream gate. Keith is yelling the encouragement. And it is like trying to drive

Riverside Park is not full, but there are many there, there and on the bridge and walking in and out of the boathouse, along the bank and up onto that railroad trestle.

As they have walked the water looking to see the river and thinking how to run their boats, I have spotted out the holes I want to shoot from. And we are ready. Quite ready.

It becomes serious now.

Watch . . . the first one out, under the gun, through the starting gate, turning, flowing, fighting, losing, winning, shifting back for number three—upriver—turning and going, the clock is ticking, the boaters are watching that one, that first one. How well, how hard does it look. The next one is started. The call is going out over the loudspeakers but it is ignored by anyone who knows the sport.

"Kast is next," that's what someone says. It is

up a good grade when ice is firm on the road. She is doing well to hold it even.

Rich Barthles is up next. Rich Barthles, a surfer who gave it up and tried to kayak and hated it and switched to a canoe and felt that right, is up next. From Los Angeles and recreation supervising for mentally retarded kids and wanting to get them boating next year, and just getting married to Teri whom you would like as a friend even as you would like Rich and who is also racing, he is poised in the water.

The man with the starting watch signals and the pistol goes off into the air and he's through that starting gate. Watch that paddle, working hard and churning the water in strained strokes. Fast and hard and like digging in, the orange canoe goes and he guides it, but it's got to be good. Through those gates not that much wider than your boat? Like riding a horse at a gallop and

135

threading a sailmaker's needle. Yeah.

Then boats and colors and watching those fiber and stinking liquid things move, tossed under a trestle—bobbing high, and hitting through a gate and moving around a bridge piling, and it looks close.

Shift your position. Watch Johnson, now, work for a gate. See that strain, watch that face, know that pull across no muscle, almost through—time, taking time, too fast, too sloppy, too slow, too much time, cut it just right—on an up river, against-the-current gate. He goes, it's frozen in time, it looks like slow motion, it's one man in one of those—things—forcing himself upon the will of the water. Digging in, the blade is a shovel. And now, almost, almost, almost through and watch, he's letting up and trying to spin it out using the current to carry him toward the next one but—no—not quite clear. Just a touch, a tiny touch, just a shoulder against the edge of the inside of the pole, just enough to make it not perfect, not right, ten more seconds on the score. What's in your mind, Johnson? Fight for it that hard, fight for that—talking of many seconds—long, about halfway through the course and have it get touched. Oh, what can you think? Only that that one is over and another is—had better be—coming up quick and concentrate on doing it.

For two days it goes on. Two days with a different river each day. For two days it goes on with two runs and that's all and that's what means you win or lose. And if the first day was a muscle course, well, the second day is beyond muscle.

Up river, up by Turquoise Lake, is a dam. The Bureau of Reclamation is cutting a tunnel across the Great Divide. Water will move through it. The work, though, is going slowly. Stockpiled is material. The stuff should have been used by now, would have been used by now had the tunneling gone as planned, but it hasn't. And water is coming out of the dam, water that would otherwise stay, water that's got to be run off to keep it from piling up over the materials. That's why the river keeps rising, steadily if slowly, every day. You can clock it in hours from the time it is let go until it hits the F Street bridge. It may be the last time the river rushes quite that fast.

So the river moves faster, the water covers more of the rocks, and washes away some of the rough white spots. The downriver run will be fast, tricky still, but fast. The slalom becomes a muscle course. Reverse it. The river is low, the wild water run is slow and constantly running over rocks—pick a path—and the slalom is quite a question of skill. If this year's race sets a record time it will probably stand as long as the dam up-river stands.

Herman Kirckhoff, Canadian National Champion, is big. He has the build of a gymnast—but a big one. Running down in a wet shirt, helmet on his head, he turns that kayak proper and so, moving fast, water juts out from his blade as he rotates it in the air. With his even, precise, movements he's looking almost like a machine, and he's breathing through his mouth. A series of yells go up, good and clear through that gate and gone from sight beyond the bridge.

I'm across the bridge myself now—looking down. Frankie Markis is starting out. The announcer says into his microphone Markis is a Salida lad. But it happens somehow; he's tipped and out and that bridge seems in the way, then the wet-suited divers are in that water and Markis is headed, slight swim, into shore, his head above the water. Quick. And he looks O.K. But I'm far off and later learn he won a broken sternum and torn cartilages for his effort. And that is part of it.

The scores say this—Cindy Goodwin won women's kayak class, Kast won K1 (Daniel third), Johnson won C1 (Barthles second), Chladek, Stan and Ema, won C2M, and Johnson and Chladek won C2. And all of that is part of it, too. But you knew that.

And for all of the people—the rest in those sixty entries—those who neither won nor were beaten up by the river, for them it was still trying and maybe doing a beautiful gate or two, or all but two. But however that went, it was for them. It was trying to do what they wanted to do. And each one knows if he won his own race or not. So there are some complaints about some judges' scoring—there almost always are, no matter what the sport—but times can never change what you did with yourself, that boat and the river. Only with what others know.

Into the blue, big pickup truck with the boat-rack on the back, along Highway 50, alongside of the Arkansas River, we go.

"Cottonwood. Known all over the world," Keith says about that bit of rapids. "Five paddle strokes and you're through."

Into the water with the canoes, a last look and feel and taste before that race.

"We'll just go through it to know how it will be. It won't change."

"They haven't had any rain here in a long time."

Then, after skipping like stones over the water, coming out—"Look at that path. It's about as wide as a downriver boat."

Keith and Linda and Rick and Teri and Walter who is jockey-size and just does not look strong enough are all here. Walter is blond headed and named Erber and is considered very good, but probably not big enough to take this. The only English he speaks is: "I do not speak English." He's Austrian.

Driving back along the road, they can talk about how to do it—with each other more like teams than competitors. Yeah. That's all right. The sun is being hidden by the mountains now and it is already becoming cold. The day ends like that— or ends for all practical purposes like that—with the truck moving back toward town, wet paddlers, boats put onto the rack following along, the air tinged with the cool sadness of the end of the day and the sun looking like a golden streak on the river water below. The water that will be tomorrow the road Highway 50 was today.

I could describe it, but I'll just say it: everybody there was tense and happy and ready and in the good kind feeling of being ready and knowing it will not be long. It was almost like the night before Christmas.

"Well," says Parks, "if you say this is man against nature I won't read your book."

"How about if I quote somebody else who says it?"

"No."

"Still not good enough, huh?"

"Well, yeah I guess it is."

We're sitting on one of the most fall-apart couches in captivity. It is leaning against the wall of the small room of the boathouse, downstairs. That's the room where Greda Kolbeck is passing out programs, information and coffee.

"See," Parks says, "I suppose there are two very different kinds of people involved in this. You've got the racers. They run into each other and reminisce. One says to the other, do you remember wave No. 43 on the national championship course? And the other one says, Oh, yes, I had planned a path around it, but it was too difficult, I nearly rolled, but that wasn't the roughest. Do you recall rapid No. 21? And that's really all they know. That's what they care about—the race, always the race. Then there are the others. And for me it's just a beautiful thing to go down a river, race or not. You're out there and away from so much and the trees, take this river for instance, the trees

are beautiful as you watch them, and the way the rocks rise up. These are things you can see in no other way. If you're not on the river and going through, you can't have the same angle. And you know how different it all looks from the road. The road isn't down there where it all starts up from. Right?"

"Right." I said. I didn't say, but maybe I should have, "Parks. I like you. And thanks."

"No, well, I don't have those little slips of paper," Greda tells the announcer.

"Well, we have to have them. We want to be able to tell the people something about the contestants."

"Oh, well," she says, "just tell them they're all nice guys."

The gun goes off. The other stuff is over. It's serious and the gun goes off and the first racer is heading downriver. Kast gets off third and moves fast, not waiting, but staking out for the lead right off.

He gets it before the first big rapids and streaks through. He is moving. And others are, too. Now just think about that, going down a river, picking out a path—and there is one way that is clearer and quicker than the others—and keeping your knees up against the boat, shifting it just so to keep its balance. The day is turning cool already and the sun just masked with clouds. The water is cold, damned cold, to the touch and it's hitting you in the face and getting into your boat even with its seals and spray shield. Now your feet and legs are cold. You have a little pumping device that should force the water out and keep you light. Time to think of a million things, but always having to think about you and the river. On and on and on and on and on and on and on and looking at water and rapids and reading the river as you go, where's that rock, how much clearance, and passing or being passed by another paddler. Time to stop? Just get carried for a minute or two or more? No, no such time, everyone has that speed—paddle that's the only way to have more. Think about the sweat underneath your nylon jacket, think about being hot through the shoulders and neck and cold on your face and legs—then smash up into the water with it slapping you in the face, and tipping your boat and still you've got to ride that out and keep going.

Cottonwood. Not far from the end of the line,

end of the race. They're coming through. I'm hunched up by the rocks farther down.

The water is heavy and heaving and dashing up over the rocks and me and my cameras. Bear Creek rapids, the first of the big rapids, was quieter this year. Tincup was the next of the landmark names and then Cottonwood just a few miles from where it all ends at the Cotopaxi bridge.

There are people here, too. They are sitting high up on the rocks that lead back to the road. We've come from the start to Bear Creek rapids, passed up Tincup and the straight, dead stretches, and come here. Logistics are not on the side of the single photographer. Still it has to be enough.

Kast comes through. He does not look that tired. He didn't look at all tired at Bear Creek. And now he is still going, paddling fast and hard down. There is a long pause and then another one comes through. It's Herman Kirckhoff. And he is still moving strong. Then Walter Erber. And the pain and the strain are on his face. He looks so exhausted I hunch there worrying about him, thinking he cannot make it, then the boat just tips and he is underwater, I watch. The eskimo roll flips it back up and over and right and he looks refreshed from the shock.

The others come through, too. How do you say how they come through—they crash, but it is not they who crash, but they only look as though they are crashing through the river because the river is carrying them along, too, just as it has carried others and other things as different and similar as bodies and wooden debris.

At the Cotopaxi bridge. Kast comes in. What can he say, what can anyone say when a newspaper man asks how do you feel? "Tired but happy." And you could tell that by looking at him.

They can do their math. Figure that time and how did it come out that way. It came out with Herman Kirckhoff, the Canadian champion, beating the old record and doing it in two hours and three minutes and six seconds. And even that wasn't good enough. Kast had beaten that record and dropped under two hours. One hour, 58 minutes and 40.9 seconds.

Walter Erber lasted. And he came in third. Gunter Hemmersbach (remember him, the German fellow who'd migrated to Detroit?) came in fourth. Stan and Ema Chladek were the only racing two-place canoe, so there was no class, but the officials

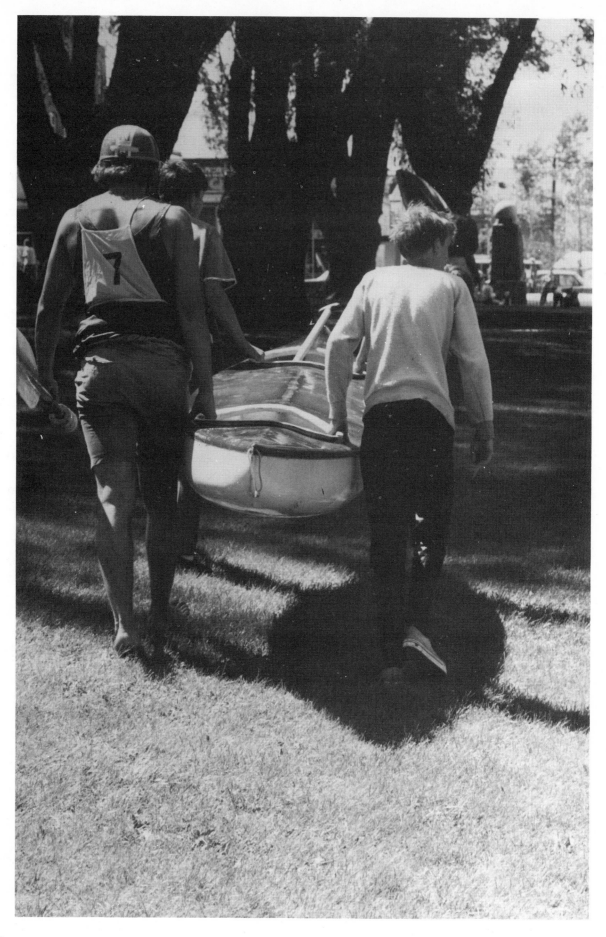

140

gave them a trophy anyway because their time of two hours, eighteen minutes and 59 seconds was quite good for a double canoe.

The river is not quiet now.

But it is empty of people. And it moves on without them. There goes a heavy log washed along in the current. And the sound of the rushing river comes up from that water. Yesterday there were women and men on it. And today it is alone. It is unchanged by that experience. Some consider victory only doing what it, itself, does each day.

On it rolls, on it rolls. On and on and on. From Turquoise Lake up beneath the Sanatch Range the water comes spilling, spilling, sliding and sloping away down the mountains, and it moves on, spilling and rushing, white and foamy and wild down and down and down past Leadville, Granite, Buena Vista, Salida and down past Wellsville, Howard and the Cotopaxi bridge. . . . and still it is not done. It is not tired. It is not finished. Not yet, it's not.

For any good man would rather take chances
any day with his life than his livelihood and
that is the main point about professionals
that amateurs seem never to appreciate.
—Ernest Hemingway

9
GRAND PRIX

Yes, here. Of course, here. Here it had to be. Or almost here. Because here is still going—running South. Down from the long night of the Freeway and the Thruway, running South with Lake Seneca by my side and the sun, not that much more than just up, running with me. Sliding along on the left, fast in—no on—the waters and slipping slowly through the sky. Then the one on the lake is behind the single line of thin trunked trees. Watching it come and go between them, broken and hidden by their bars, but breaking free over the gray lake, and watching itself from the gray sky.

Then on and through what stands to be taken for a town and into another of the same and call it Watkins Glen.

So I've come to this town that looks like a broken-down pair of boots, this town that says of itself resort where resort needn't say pleasure. And there is the feel of the pull—if not destiny, then of knowledge? Or is it something less yet more real than that? But whatever it is, I am here and poised on the edge of a forest of visions and the sun is still stuck low in the sky and the day is cold to those not yet used to losing summer. And if you've come with me the wind is hard up against your face as you stand, past the town now, and look along the quiet, gray strip of pavement that seems smaller and simpler than the road you left back home.

But it is a road you can admire and seems more true than most, for it winds and wraps around this piece of the world and comes back to stop upon itself in the place where it has started. And today it is empty, but tomorrow and the day after that and the day after that it will fill with automobiles and drivers who have come to ride upon it. And for three days it will become the place of the Grand Prix—the great prize. And that is why you have come.

For us this is a final place, a stopping point, a destination that is not a destination but only a high, clear stance which offers a better view of the road—perhaps the best such view.

There are others, though, who have come to it as one more stop in a long line of just such stops. These are the ones I have come to watch, and they have come from Johannesburg and Jaramo, Monte Carlo and Spa, Zandvoort and Clermont-Ferrand, Brands Hatch and Hockenheim, Osterreichring and Monza and Mont Tremblant. From places with a quotient of magic in their names. And these men, too, are made at least a little of just such magic.

But this time there is one who shall not come, and by his absence make this race a duel with a dead man.

The others who had come to race knew this—intimately. For me, it thrust the scene into the symbolic. And it seemed to serve as a constant

reminder of our common future. To live seems easy and to die seems simple, but to live knowing you will die and to die knowing you will not live seems neither simple nor easy nor fun. But only true.

Such knowledge goes with their game. The rest of us must catch it where we can. And there are very few who play their game. That too, is a part of its nature.

At this time it is a sport you speak of in terms of a dozen or two. Although they come from four continents, there are only about two dozen regular professional racers. There are no more than a dozen manufacturers of their cars, fewer teams, a handful of privateers, and only 13 Grand Prix races, each of which, at this time, must be set in a different country, and so reach from Africa across Europe to the three countries of the North American continent.

The sport is limited by circumstance, and perhaps a little by design. But there are never very many at the top, and this is the top. The car is called Formula I and it is built to a standard formula which defines the class. And it is an automobile, a highly bred mechanical mount that has been refined and almost perfected. It does better than any other automobile what an automobile is supposed to do—move over roads. And it does that with glamor and grace and poise. It is not the fastest, the biggest, the handiest, safest or most durable automobile. But it does not have to be.

Other sport cars are defined by the sport. Dragsters are defined by rapid acceleration through a clear straight strip, off-road racers are defined by conditions of speed and endurance away from pavement, oval track cars by the ovalness of the track. Only road racing machines are defined by

The title is awarded on a point system, not unlike that used by the rodeo cowboys. The season is divided, roughly, in half and a driver can throw out his worst place in each of the halves. The points run: winner–9, second place–6, third place–4, fourth place–3, fifth place–2, and sixth place–1.

There is a similar point scale, and competition for championship for constructors.

With such cars, such drivers and such a title it would be strange if the sport were not coated in glamor. It certainly is. But I was standing with some other photographers as we waited, in the high, cold wind, for the race to start. We talked about how much of the glamor seems manufactured from misunderstanding, fantasy and—perhaps—hope. What we didn't really understand until later was that glamor, much more than anything else, lies within the viewer. And, since all glamor is an illusion, it is impossible to scrub it away by simply reciting the facts. And, in this case, some of the

the nature of the automobile, and only then does the nature of the sport work to redefine the machine. And that redefinition moves up from the salon and sports cars through the various formulas until it reaches Formula I.

Just as these automobiles exist at the top of the essence of the automobile, the drivers exist at the top of their profession. The Grand Prixs they run moves one toward the title of world champion driver.

It is the same as with the cars. Grand Prix road-racing requires a concentrated combination of driving disciplines. There must be rapid and fearfully accurate braking, accelerating, cornering from right and left, passing, climbing, shifting and steering. The races are run in sun, mist, rain and fog. There can be water, mud or even sand on the course. There is room at the top only for the best of drivers. And only the best of these will be marked as world champions.

facts reinforce the illusion. The simple situation is that just as photographers are becoming the cavaliers of communication, so Grand Prix drivers are replacing or have already replaced matadors as the cavaliers of sport. And they have always moved close to that position.

Before Barney Oldfield got off his bicycle, stuck his cigar in his teeth and started driving for Ford, a new class of men had already been begun. In 1895. Then the first motor race was run from Paris to Bordeaux to Paris. And that makes Emile Levassor the first man to win a motor race. These city to city races flourished until 1903 when frantic French officials stopped the Paris–Madrid run at Bordeaux because of accidents and malfunctions. But already closed raceways were being set up. And one would be more than ready to go that very year for the Gordon Bennet trophy races. The scene was already shifting. But open road racing was a long way from through.

In 1907 the Paris newspaper *Le Matin* decided to test the automakers' boast that "as long as a man has a car he can do anything and go anywhere." So they challenged the world to provide the men and machines to race from Peking to Paris. Allen Andrews offers an after-the-fact account of their adventures under the title *The Mad Motorists*. Too apt. And what adventures they were as cars were dragged over the mountains, pushed across the deserts, cleared as special trains and driven over Trans-Siberian tracks. What a race. What men. What machines—the biggest, driven by the winner, was a 40-horsepower Itala. It left Peking on June 10 and reached Paris on August 10. And its journey, and even more the others, was an almost unbelievable fact which came perilously close to ending in the death of drivers and passengers. And against it all ran the current of minor espionage and confidence trickery as one team tried to outdo the others.

Politics unsettled the contest, but it provided such vivid reading that the idea was expanded a little later into a New York to Paris race. A race by way of China.

Though it was a grand scheme, it was something less than an automobile race. Often the cars were more like a relay-race baton which had to be pushed or carried by the teams and their employees. If it proved that the men could make it, and if it proved that the cars could make it,

it still did not prove that the cars could make it carrying the men. The fault, though, really fell to the lack of roads, supplies and navigational precision. Still it seems to me that both races, and especially the first, were grand experiments undertaken in a spirit of innocence that can never be really recovered.

Even before these races started, the French had hit upon a place and a term that were to become classic in the motor racing world. They offered the Grand Prix of France, the first race so called, in 1906, and held it at Le Mans. The movement would continue from that time until now—more firmly fixing the course as rather regular roadway, about two cars wide. The Germans would eventually manufacture such a roadway just for racing. And it would become legend as a track—the Nurbehring. Later the United States would follow with Watkins Glen. Where we stand now: a narrow, gray-white line that leads through the land. Grass, trees, mud and rails and fences stand still by its sides as it twists around upon itself. Though it's different than the dust-packed stretch from Paris to Bordeaux, and Bordeaux to Paris, it is still very much the same.

The men too are different, but a lot the same. Take Ralph DePalma, perhaps the best of the early racers; he was more the individual than the team man. He resigned from the American Mercer group in protest when they hired Barney Oldfield. And he didn't stop there. He entered a decrepit Mercedes in the Vanderbilt Cup Race held the year the war would start in Europe. And he skillfully held a place and moved consistently around the track as Oldfield kept feeling the pressure to stop for tire changes. De Palma was coming up late in the duel and signaled his crews he was headed in for an oil change the next lap. Oldfield smiled to himself and stopped for new tires. De Palma, of course, didn't. Oldfield caught all but a couple of hundred yards up. It is reported that he did not appreciate the humor of the situation.

Tazio Nuvolari would have. He is, perhaps, my personal favorite. In thirty years of racing he made it plain where he wanted to stop—first. He piled up over 150 wins but only about 17 second places. For Nuvolari, in his life and his racing, it was all or nothing. And it was going to be all in 1935. The Nazis were banking on a victory at their own Nurbehring. Manfred von Brauchitsch

—what a delightfully Prussian sounding name for a red-haired man—was sitting sternly behind the wheel of his gleaming Mercedes. Nuvolari arrived with a beaten-up Alfa. A master of cornering, and a man whom some said had too much courage, Nuvolari all but ignored the fog and went slipping around the curves, edging ever more dangerously close to the trees that waited to catch the car of the careless driver. But he pushed himself into second place. And those who saw him that day insisted he was a man protected either by a god or a devil. He stopped in hard behind Brauchitsch and held there, 12 seconds back, but kept the edge and started to nudge. The Mercedes moved with less precision, its driver, perhaps becoming more concerned with the little Alfa than his own driving, tried to push it. The gamble worked. The Mercedes had been pushed too far. A tire gave out and Nuvolari won.

Incidentally, Nuvolari had driven that race with his right leg wrapped in a cast.

While some racers built their legends on the track, others added to theirs off of it. Some were like Harry Schell, an American in Paris whose idea of work was hiring out as a tail gunner for Finland during the Russo-Finnish War and whose

idea of fun was driving a racing car. He drove his last one in 1970—he died after a crash during practice. Others are like Graham Hill. The two-time world champion walks along the pits in an incredible limping, broken-up walk. His hair, long to accommodate the style, moves him further out of time and further into place so that it is hard not to see some many-tried leader of Condittoarie strolling away after a chat with the Doge of Venice. But he was looking, in fact, at the place where—one year earlier—he had been thrown out of his car as it rolled away from the track. after a rear tire came loose at about 150 miles per hour. Both legs were seriously broken, and a knee dislocated. Hill, bound up in casts, was relieved enough that the doctors had stopped short of amputation. But not relieved enough to simply sit, so, around December, he convinced John Coombs to lash a swivel chair on a land rover so they could get in a day of shooting.

But behind the legends and stories, what is a race driver? A race driver is Jackie Stewart. The title holder at the Glen, Stewart was out of the running for a repeat. He is five feet six inches tall and weighs about 148 pounds. His taste is now, his fashion current and expensive, his hair to his shoulders. He looks as much in place under a grouse helmet holding a fly-rod as wrapped in flame-proof neo-armor and stepping into a Formula I racer. His father ran a garage in Scotland, near Dumbarten, and his brother became a professional driver. Jackie wasn't interested in following. He spent his time skeet shooting and eventually won championship titles from Ireland, Wales and England and finished as runner-up for Britain's Olympic Team. He has said that Bruce McLaren was partly responsible for getting him into auto racing, and he started at Charterhall where Jim Clark, another Scot of note, had started his career. It moved from there. Stewart had the requirements and the talent. He soon had the desire to race as well. He was light, had good eyes, fast reflexes, and the type of steel-hard concentration that keeps the moments of braking, shifting and accelerating through each foot of the track firmly fixed in his mind, and ready to be summoned up. In 1964 he entered the Continental competitions and moved into a London flat with Clark—a couple of Scots if not after the world, then after the world title. Clark got it twice. And then, in the rain, in 1968, in Hockenheim, Clark's Lotus-Cosworth skidded. And Clark was dead. In 1970 McLaren was killed. But Stewart goes on. He was caught in his own crack-up at the Belgian Grand Prix of 1966, and waited, trapped, for more than half an hour as the gasoline rose higher on his chest.

His actions since then have become truly professional. In 1969 he almost single-handedly closed down the Belgian Grand Prix. He insisted it was entirely too dangerous to run on the wet track. He started using a seat belt, insisting his BRM Formula I be outfitted with one. He was, incidentally, the first Formula I driver to do that. Others have followed. He has fought for the required installation of special remote-control fire extinguishers on the cars. And he has rebuffed

critics who claim he's destroying the "sport" by suggesting that the older, casual approach is more a sign of irresponsibility than guts.

And his attitude toward engaging risk has come down to this simple statement: "I don't get my kicks from flirting with death. I flirt with life."

Now if you have never played this game, either by accident or design, ask one who has and understands and he can explain. And, even if he can't, he knows. And a little part of that is this: death defines our lives. For some to know this is enough to demand some of what they want from their time of existence. For others the knowing is only a part of the process. Or, as Disraeli once suggested, "Experience is the child of Thought, and Thought is the child of Action. We cannot learn men from books." We cannot learn ourselves from books, either. Stewart has found one way to learn.

And that is a driver. A driver is also Jackie Oliver. Born in the early 1940s, he came to racing from Essex and moved up through club matches. The Lotus spotters watched him racing their Elans and a Brabham F3, liked his style and hired him to race for them, moving him up in 1968 to race Formula I cars. He's also short and light. He looks pleasant enough and if he's reading his own reviews, he knows he's being considered as a possible contender.

And a driver is Jack Brabham. At the Glen, this time, he is 44 years old. The oldest of all. And he started racing almost a quarter of a century before in the dirt of Australia, where he comes from. And he pushed his way into Formula I competition. Brabham, unlike the others, seems less the adventurer than the businessman. And in a way that's right. His business is racing, and he's won the championship three times, two years straight, and the third time in his own car, called a Brabham-Repco. He was the first man to win a Grand Prix in a car of his own design and construction. But with the good has come in the bad. In a different business they might call it a slow season. And 1968 was the slowest of the slow. At season's end, Brabham looked at his name on the point standings chart and saw it second from last. Not only Brabham, but his whole team was jinxed. He finished one race that season, his partner two. He stayed in the business and thought 1969 might be a better year. It might have been. But Brabham was running tire tests just before the French Grand

Prix. He went off the road on a corner—and calculates the speed midway through the turn at 113 mph—and sat there, out of sight of the pits with his leg stuck so that his foot jammed down the throttle and kept the engine revving. The instruments were twisted into obscurity and he couldn't switch off the machine. He finally killed it and sat waiting, wondering if the fuel that spilled out of the ruptured tank would ignite.

He activated the fire extinguisher against the possibility and waited about a half an hour for someone to notice he was gone and get him out of his trap.

With it all, the only damage to Brabham was a badly broken left ankle. He came back with an automatic transmission Zodiac for the British Grand Prix and drove with his left leg resting on a pile of pillows. And that, also, is a driver.

And it is the driver along with the car and

the track that you hear about. Then it is Sunday, cold and windy, and I walk through that, unhappily, from my car in the paddock lot up to the Tech Center and, flashing my pass, go into it and stand there just a bit inside the door watching the men move in the inside darkness that isn't totally disturbed by the incandescent lighting. And I get warm. Here is another part of it. Here is an important part of it. Dunlop people in gold-

is a race, too. Developments move so fast that the company which had the winning tire in South Africa has been out-worked by Monaco and will come back in by France. And these people are against one long wall of this mid-morning tech center. Away from that wall, the open area is divided by wooden stalls. None of the stalls are empty. Many have mechanics in them. In dirty red, aqua and gold coveralls the mechanics move rather quietly about the racing engines and work to make them run. Five men come in from the back door. They are walking regularly, a stocky, cocky one leading the others. They look, perhaps, like factory workers showing up in Edinburgh. A tall, lanky one gets into his dark blue uniform first, the stocky one finds the connection for his light and the corner stall brightens a bit. The tarps are pulled loose and the blue car with the white JACKIE STEWART lettering emerges.

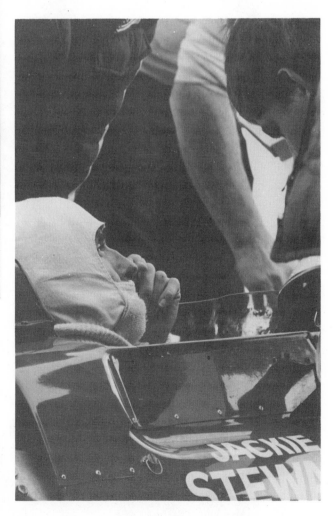

yellow knit shirts spin tires and stand behind stacks of them talking quickly with each other. Each driver would tell you that the tires you use for a given day at a given track can mean the difference between a win and second place. They are that important. And, on this morning, the men of the tire manufacturers are working with their product. They come from Goodyear and Firestone and Dunlop. At this time, no one else is offering tires to the Formula I racers. And theirs

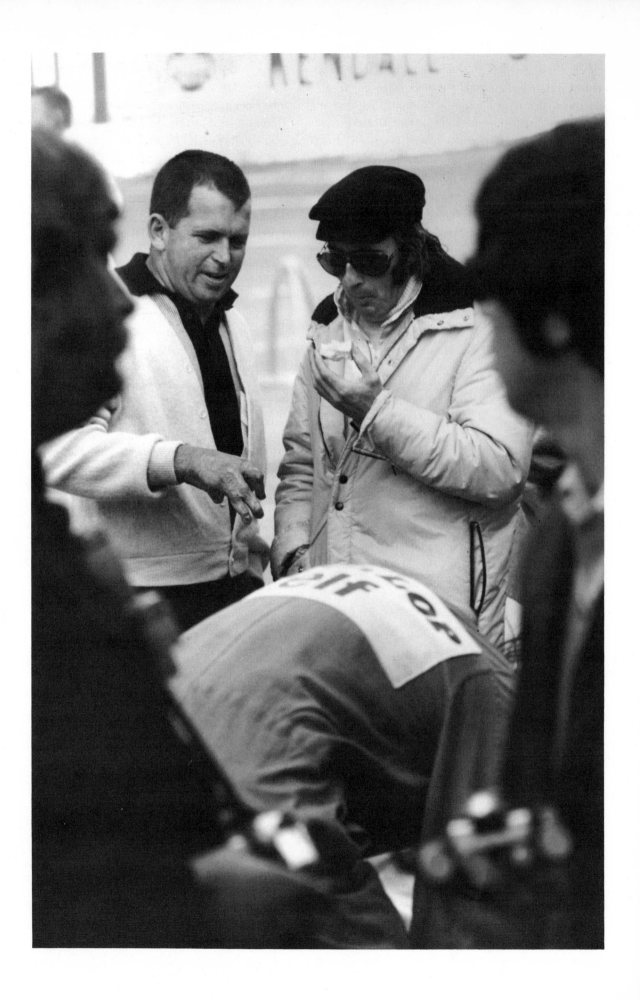

The pit crews are to this racing what the ground crews were to the RAF at the Battle of Britain. And they get about as much notice. But they, too, have reached a peak of a profession. It's easy to think they get the fringe benefits with their job. After all they'll travel through three continents before the season is over. But, as one says, the inside of any garage looks pretty much like the inside of any other.

up to their top form and make them all come together just right. Some of these gentlemen have become legends, too. Alfred Neubauer, the Mercedes-Benz manager during the 1930s, built an image out of iron discipline, steel will and a flint tongue. Colin Chapman, who with Pete Warris is still serving as manager of Lotus, started out building cars, then racing them and finally got a passenger's ride on a Formula I—Jim Clark was

Ken Tyrrell is stalking around, his head ducked down, under what appears to be a gray Gannex cloth and wool cap. His nose is hawkish. His mouth dips down. And he seems so concerned he looks like he might break if you talked to him. He's another part—the team manager. In this case of the Tyrrell Racing Organization. And he's a man with what must seem like a million concerns. If he's like much of anything else—especially in producer Tyrrell's case—he is like a film director. It's his job to get the best elements, bring them

steering it into the winner's circle, and it was a double ring ceremony. While Clark took the driver's title, Chapman picked up the Constructor's Championship. But, no matter how expensive and professional the sport has become, there is room for Rob Walker. A member of the Johnny Walker Scotch Whiskey Walkers, he is one of the last capital S Sportsmen in it. He is independent—a privateer. And, according to legend, the occupation blank on his passport is filled by the word "Gentleman." At the Glen, Graham Hill would

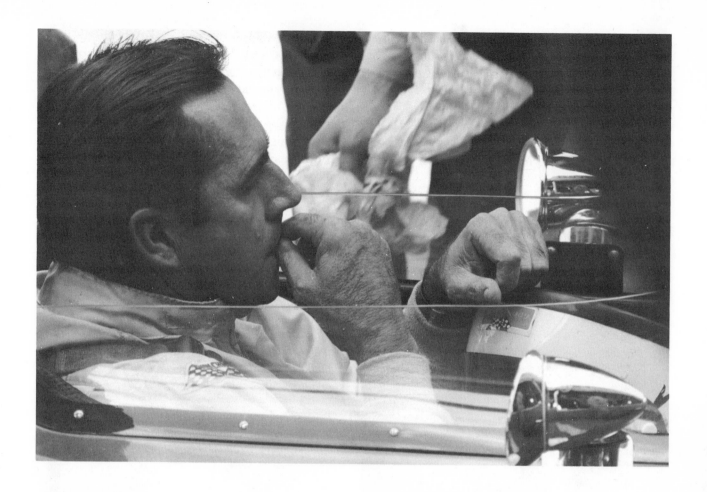

drive Walker's entry—Lotus-Ford.

By the way, prize money is awarded not to drivers, in Grand Prixs, but to their managers. And the percentage split varies from team to team year to year—but it's been suggested that even a 50–50 division would be quite high for the driver.

And, since we're talking about money, quite a few drivers don't make enough in a season to put them in the upper middle class bracket. And it's a safe assumption that a pushy life insurance salesman can make more than all but a very few.

Time trials, in the pits, drivers and managers and mechanics stand and look troubled and concerned talking, standing near or over the cars looking like architects and engineers puzzling over blueprints. The trials set lap times that place the cars in the starting positions, the fastest on the pole and moving back to the slowest starting in last place. So it's to their advantage to place well. But it is more than that, much more—it's a time to test the cars on that track, to test tires, to see if the new designs and ideas are working, and if the old ones will keep coming through.

The drivers are suited, and to see them is to make the comparison between this place and time and knights. One lifts the visor of his helmet and then pulls it off. Instead of chain mail, his head is still covered, but in a flame-proof guard. His gloves are gauntlets, his suit complete. They're helped into their mounts by some of the closest things to squires left in sports.

The timers, with watches and blank forms, move to the edge of the track; they'll keep their records and watch the performance and wait, and wonder if they can make it work well enough for tomorrow or the day after that.

The stalls are filled with tools and tires and people who have come to work or just to watch. The cars sit, small and incredibly low, as wrenches tighten belts, and aviation is funneled into their tanks. And so it goes through one day and on and into the next. All necessary. All preliminary. All meaning nothing except as it serves to mean something for the race. The race. The race is all—or almost all.

The rain didn't stop. It changed. To hail. And that meant I'd figured wrong, all wrong. By the track at time trials, I'd been waiting for the cars to pass a special corner, and decided that I'd not pick up my slicker, but stay and shoot it out before they went in. I got one, thought another was coming around and the hail started—not all that big but hard enough. I crouched in the shelter of a pickup-truck-camper and crammed my cameras back into their bag. Then I strolled back to my car, got in and lit a cigarette.

Sun. Shift to rain. Shift to hail. That's Fall— Summer losing to Winter. They fight it out twice each year, and every time you know who will win, but they fight it out as if the outcome were still uncertain. It becomes beautiful that way. Beautiful and powerful and somehow right.

The cars, of course, are off the track. . . . So I just sit there smoking my cigarette and wondering

what the drivers are doing back in the pits right now. But even as twilight is a time for summing up the day, so fall seems a time for summing up the year—and, with one more race left, it would be an appropriate time to sum up this season.

It had started a long, long time ago, in March in South Africa. And just everybody was supposed to be there. Everybody was supposed to be there, in fact, with new cars. And everybody but Lotus made it. They did have a new top driver though, or sort of had. Last year Jochen Rindt had been labeled No. 1, but with Graham Hill now on the team, the numbering didn't seem appropriate. Maybe it should have. After last season, Jackie Stewart singled Rindt out as the man who he'd have to keep beating to win. Rindt does move right along, on the track and in his career. In 1963 he raced Formula Junior, in 1964 it was Formula II and then he started on Formula I, winding up in 1969 as a Lotus driver. It was not a good year for Lotus or Rindt. But everybody knew who he was and what he could do. And it was just a question of time. But then, it is always a question of time, isn't it? Time, or the times, made him an Austrian—and so sparked Austrian interest in the sport, again. Rindt's father was German and born in Germany. His parents were both killed in a 1943 air-raid and he went to live with his Austrian mother's parents. But that was then and now it was March and he was in South Africa.

Jacky Ickx was there, too, and in his new Ferrari. Ickx's father was a motoring journalist, and the son emerged as someone to write about. By the time he was 16 he was racing motorbikes. At twenty he was racing cars and ran on to the Ferrari team in 1968. In 1969 he teamed with Jack Brabham and won enough points to finish second to Stewart.

Stewart moved off first and fastest in the Kyalami run and watched Ickx move into second. Jack Brabham was laying back, but moved hard enough to pass Stewart and keep running for the win.

Lotus brought out their new cars—called 72s—for the Spanish Grand Prix. This didn't help. Jackie Stewart, as was becoming his custom, moved into the lead. Jackie Oliver had a malfunction in his suspension and hit Ickx's Ferrari broadside, splitting open the gasoline tanks and sparking a fire. Oliver got out in time, Ickx was burned on his arms and legs. But he was alive, and moving. The Yardly-BRM team ordered Pedro Rodriguez in after Oliver's mishap, because his car could have been flawed too. Brabham, as was becoming his custom, moved into Stewart territory but he was pushing too hard this time. His car couldn't handle it and the engine died.

Johnny Servoz-Gavin wound up with fifth place and a hunch. The tough little Frenchman wanted out of racing. And, since getting out of anything alive is mostly a question of knowing when to get out, his hunch was fully respected. He did not race again.

Then on to the first of the truly traditional Grand Prixs—Monte Carlo. A course set in the streets of the Mediterranean capital of gambling and grace. One hundred laps of all but constant shifting, braking and accelerating. Go and less than two miles later be back there, going again. Ninety-nine times more. Ninety-eight. Seventy-three to go and it happened again. Stewart had been leading. Car trouble slowed him. Brabham into the lead. Still familiar?

But back, and not that far, is Jochen Rindt. No new Lotus this day. None needed. He's moving, slipping and gripping around the tiny course, but how much time can you make up? There are only two answers possible—enough and not enough. Enough would put him past Brabham, but Brabham is pushing out too. And so they go, Brabham and Rindt, into the last lap, the last hairpin turn. But there it is. Brabham is sliding, slow, slipping straight into a barrier.

Rindt is past.

Brabham gets back to the track.

Rindt rides into the winner's circle.

The new Lotus was ready, and right, for Holland. Rindt moved out front early and you could tell that if he could keep going he had it. And how he had it. He lapped everybody but Stewart.

But from the 23rd lap on, Rindt, and Stewart and all of the others had a landmark. It was a column of smoke and flame lifting up beside the track. It was the burning car of Piers Courage.

And Courage was dead.

Ickx led in France until his car went out with electrical troubles. Then Beltoise led until he came in with a flat tire. Then Rindt led. And he kept leading right up to the last.

Then Brands Hatch for the Grand Prix of Britain. Ickx led. Out with transmission troubles. This time Rindt was right behind and took the lead. Brabham was in second and moving hard to catch up. Then stayed just back, riding Rindt, waiting for the first mistake. He waited for more than three-fourths of the race but it happened. Rindt muffed a shift and Brabham ripped along side and pushed for all he had to get a lead. He got one. And one lap to go. And here comes the winning car and it's a Lotus and Rindt is at the wheel and where is Brabham and here he comes but not racing, now, just rolling. Out of gas. Coasting to second.

The Nurbehring, like Monte Carlo, is a course with a history. Too much perhaps. It has been the site of the German Grand Prix since 1926, with one year of interruption. This year it got its second interruption—to Hockenheim. The place where Jimmy Clark was killed.

And it looked like Hockenheim could be rough. Twenty-one cars started. Seven finished. Rindt was the first of the seven. Ickx came in second. He had been right back there, but Rindt's mistake never came. And Ickx undoubtedly knew it was better for his team to have a Ferrari finish second than not at all, so when Clay Regazzoni took his Ferrari in with a broken gearbox, Ickx was all they had left.

Rindt was now well ahead in points. Five point races to go and the next one was the Austrian Grand Prix. And it had been revived, in part, because of Rindt. And here he is, ready to go first, sitting in that pole position. But he didn't get away quite right. Regazzoni moved into the lead. Then Ickx passed him. Rindt was moving along in third. But Francois Cevert could change some of that. His car, one of Tyrrell's, looked—and I gather sounded—like it had had a massive hemorrhage and was vomiting oil onto the track, and into the air. He slowed Hulme and Brabham and then Rindt, when his car slipped on the slick spots. Maybe it didn't matter though. Rindt dropped out a little later, his engine finished. And Brabham caught a rock in his radiator, which ended his attack. It stopped with one-two Ferrari as Ickx led Regazzoni across the line. Rolf Stommelen moved in third.

But Rindt might make the next one just fine. Colin Chapman intended to enter a turbine car

for Rindt at Monza. He changed his mind and they arrived with the 72s. Rindt didn't make that race, though. On Sept. 5, during a practice run, Jochen Rindt died. There was no apparent cause for the accident and it was explained only as unexplainable. All of the Lotus 72s were recalled in case the fatal flaws were hidden somewhere within them. Even Rob Walker's Lotus (which Hill would have driven) was scratched.

In 1954 Alberto Ascari, who had been a world champion driver, joined the Lancia team. He survived a bad crash in Monaco, only to be killed several weeks later while test driving a Ferrari at Monza—this same Monza. Lancia withdrew their cars, gave them to Ferrari and quit the racing game.

Lotus would be back.

Rindt wouldn't.

But his 45 points, acquired in five wins in the five races he finished, left him at the top. Regazzoni won in Italy and Ickx in Canada and it was Watkins Glen. If Ickx could take the next two, last two, with wins he'd outscore Rindt and be the world champion. For Ickx it was a duel with a dead man.

The sun had come back out, and I started thinking about walking the track, picking up shots as the cars went through their practice laps. After all, there is almost always something to do or think about doing.

I was walking now, with the groundlings, who had paid the incredibly high—or what I would consider incredibly high—entrance fee and had not paid the additional rates for the grandstands which were priced in accordance with their view of the course. Getting into a pair of very good grandstand seats at the Glen could have cost you $50 that year. But I was walking along in the paths of the groundlings now and there it was different. There you were in the infield and could move around to the different points on the track and watch the cars pass and see them cornering, coming out and hitting the straightaway. Now, as you walked along behind the fences you could watch these semi-spectators twisting, slipping, grabbing branches and each other as they made their way over the very slick mud. It had been raining off and on in this part of the state for several days. So far it had only rarely interfered with the racing, but it made the grounds where the cars were

parked, where the tents were set up, where the campers on pick-up trucks were temporarily homes, slick and soggy and cold. When the sun was out it added enough warmth of its own to make the going comfortable.

I drove up the hill and into the paddock area early on Sunday morning. It was cooler out there than it had been coming through town. The wind was higher and freer. Sitting, for a few minutes, in my car looking at the people and the place I knew it would be a very long day.

There goes a spectator, unlike most spectators. Those who have come to follow this clear through are as much participants in their own fair as watchers. Struggling against the cold, he walked along wrapped to the nose in an old army blanket. Another moved along a little behind that one, looking warm in a parka. I was envious.

Standing outside, I zipped a wool plaid cruiser over my shirt. And belted a trench-coat over that. It was still cold. I walked along the roadways to see what was happening. There were mechanics in the tech center, there were people on the grounds, but what it was all about was off in the distance of the afternoon.

By the time the blue and red and gold and other colored cars were rolled into position, the grandstands were nearly crowded, and people stood along the track. Photographers were low and high. Writers were working away inside the press building, and the clouds kept rolling, cold and gray and full of the threat of rain, across the sky. Crews had been debating whether to run on rain tires or dry tires. Finally everyone had decided on the dry tires and hoped the weather would hold.

The one who would start it was ready and waiting. He stood along the starting line. His hair was short, his hat western and his suit white. The suit was covered with patches of races past. A couple of still photographers and a motion-picture man moved in on him to get some posed flag waving—green and checkered. For a moment he would be the center of attention. Into the big-time because his hand was wrapped around the handle of a colored piece of cloth. They posed him ever so properly, but it looked like a bad shot from where we were standing, high up and looking down.

But then it was real, and he was revving his flag and dropping it as he jumped into a flat-footed landing and sort of sprinted to the side. So terribly dishonestly real it was as the cars in an expression of beauty and power raced past the man. But, fortunately for all of us, there were men in those cars. Men moving with them and making them move right. And so they were not past all men, but only some. And that's as it seems it should be.

Ickx grabbed off the pole position but Stewart, next to him, got into the lead and looked like he planned to stay there. Obviously Ickx didn't want it that way. It was here and Mexico City for him. And a win both places, or else. The field was short Rindt's Lotus, but he was there, just the same. He was there.

And there are twenty-four cars heading around that first lap of the track, and they are all in the market for the same thing. To drive well, and come in to win or close to a win, a driver has to hang his car right on the edge. He has to be going fast enough to get every bit of energy out of the machine, and he has to be going slow enough to stick to the road. And he has to know, know exactly where that thin line is. The speed

he conjures up, like a magician, to beat his competitors comes from the way he takes his corners. There the battle, the education, the endeavor is all. There the races are won or lost. The shifting must be flawless, and the braking must be right. To push the time down, you brake later. Not much later because this is a game played in parts of seconds. You brake six feet later, the length of an almost tall man, and it gets you around the corner and gives you more time to accelerate on the straight and drive up your distance. But you don't just brake late. You accelerate early. You hit the gas before you're through the corner, while you're still twisting and you know how fast to hit it, to get it going fast but not to go fast without the corner and rocket right off the road. You know that, and you do it that way. You brake as hard as you can and accelerate as good as you know how, and you shift just right at just the right times and you make it all mean something; you're watching the others and you're checking your gauges, and you're reading the messages from the pits to you, and you're aware of just how that road goes, every yard of it, and not ever knowing—not ever really knowing—if your car is going to malfunction, if this is going to be your last race, if this is where the world stops for you. You are aware. Every bit of you is aware. You're reaching out and pulling information into your mind. And you know you can botch it. If you stop at the wrong time to think about your mother or your brother or how your foot hurts you know it can be all over—you can brake just a bit too late, accelerate just a bit too early, miss a gear, get out of the groove you wanted to run in. And

you can get passed by someone who was thinking only about the race. And at this Glen 110,000 people were spread around that track watching you work.

The cars sound strange—not a buzzing, not a humming, not a roar, but their own very special sound—a high-tuned proper sound. A scream, yet not a scream. One hundred and eight times around the track, with 110,000 watching. There is a magnetic attraction that keeps such races from going boring the way so many others do. There is a pull from the sound, and the sickening smell, and the beauty and color of the cars, that keeps it from going boring. But it is something hard to watch. I have started so many Joseph Conrad books, never to finish them, but he is still a first-rate writer to me, and because I cannot finish them does not diminish him, or what he says, only sometimes it is too much. And so, without trying to understand what he means I read some more, enjoying only the graceful way he does it, but then I feel that is not enough and somehow unfair, and stop, leaving the book lay open on a table or a chair until someone else cleans that room of the house and lifts the book, and tucks it away on the bookshelves where I can find it later and try again. I could have the same trouble with Stephen Crane but his good stories do not run 200 pages or 108 laps.

But things are changing in this race. Stewart's car looks bad, it puffs up colored smoke and it seems to sound quite strange.

Eventually he is out and Ickx is in. Stewart walks the long walk from his car back to the pits. Pedro Rodriguez, a Mexican, brings his BRM

into first and keeps it rolling, right there sixteen, seventeen, eighteen laps and it looks like he's got it. But then he's into the pits on the next to last lap. He was out of fuel. And who is it who's just passed him? The question makes the rounds. Who can it be? Is it Wissel? Where's Amon?

And if you know you're smiling because it's a Lotus 72 and Emerson Fittipaldi is driving. And almost nobody has thought about him before. You have because of your own curious introduction to Brazil and karting. You see Fittipaldi is a Brazilian. Like Ickx, his father is a motor racing writer, but instead of bikes he broke in on karts. And when he broke out of South America into the International competitions in Europe he moved in about a year through the stages: from Formula Ford through Formula 3 and 2 into the race of world champions. Watkins Glen was his first win and his fourth attempt. He picked a good place

to start. With a quarter of a million dollars tied up in prize money, it was the richest such race in history. The winner's cut was $50,000.

Before he was off the platform in the winner's circle the Associated Press typewriters were banging out the lead—"There is a new South American star on the International road racing scene and he may be cut from the same mold as the great Manuel Fangio, who won five world titles."

But on that platform, in that squared circle, Fittipaldi stood and smiled and spoke in English. And part of what he said was that he was glad he could do it. He thought Jochen would have wanted it just that way.

The go Ferrari signs were gone now.

As I walked away from the crowd that had stood in front, and around Fittipaldi, a young man was holding a simply lettered black card. In white, the letters spelled out, "Jochen Rindt Lives."

That is less than certain.

But what is certain is that for the first time, a dead man was world champion driver.

That was very certain.

I drove out of there that night, up and back onto the Thomas E. Dewey Thruway. Yes. And there were a lot of us there. In the dark it was only the moving of lights, but it was not open and I missed the West, and soon the lights in front were not moving at all, but simply staying stationary and some were blinking, those high up on a bus, two buses and I slowed and moved into a position expecting a wreck. There was none. It was simply, simply mile upon mile of automobiles, inching like worms across the concrete. Two clogged lanes, not stopped but slowed to the edge of stopping and that's the way it was all the way along that line of Thruway until you reached a point of construction where cars must form a single line and move more slowly past the reconstruction of roadway that was left undone.

But the news is on the radio, and a sportscaster tells us that Emerson Fittipaldi has run to a win in the 248 mile Grand Prix of the United States at an average speed of 126.79 miles per hour.

A couple of sentences and it's over.

He did not tell us about Rindt.

Pythagoras used to say life resembles the Olympic Games; a few men strain their muscles to carry off a prize; others bring trinkets to sell to the crowd for a profit; and some there are (and not the worst) who seek no further advantage than to look at the show and see how and why everything is done. They are spectators of other men's lives in order to better judge and manage their own.—Michel de Montaigne

10
SUNDAY

And this too is Sunday. Sunday—almost Monday—with everyone else asleep, even the two tomcats who've picked out a chair apiece and the puppy who, at three months, is nearly knee-high and still puppy-noisy in his sleep. Outside it is cold. The wind drives the sound of cold through the walls of the old house. The wind is moaning in the night—a widow wind, weeping.

In the morning it had been cold, and the wind hard and fierce-harsh as I strode down the bank and twisted with the path out onto the sand by the river. The cold drove itself up against my face as I set the cans upon the log. And the wind and I became accustomed to each other—out there where only the wind had been—and I took no more notice of her.

The pistol cracked and sent out its burnt-powder smell as I popped the cans off the log and bounced them along on the sand. And it stopped, slide open, with a whisper of smoke clinging to the chamber. But the wind took that, too.

A hundred rounds. And then it was too cold.

And that's Sunday, too.

Coming in the front door—over the porch board flooring into the hall and back, through the warm, to the coffee pot. Big cup. Strong. Holding the body, not the handle in my hands, I sipped it—as is—but you could slip some whiskey or brandy in it, too.

And that is Sunday.

Rose and Rick, and later Randy can ask how it went, and you can say you've improved a lot and that it was cold, but you cannot tell about the smell of the burnt powder nor about how the wind made your face feel real nor how the simple act of hitting the targets was a small sort of satisfaction and a doing something at least all right for the amount of time you've worked on it nor how that bought you the day.

Quiet and Sunday morning with the sun up and the cold out and a lot of winter-is-here gray. Warm and nice and paid for by having finished these dispatches a couple of days before and, today, by just getting out into it and practicing with only 100 rounds. And now the day is paid for and can be enjoyed, so that, hating winter, it is impossible not to love it, too.

And then the day is one and it is late and the

big room is full of the just-chilled warmth. The Norm Thompson turtleneck had started out navy and was faded to dusk, and the old wide wale corduroy trousers were loose threads and patches and closer to white than tan, and the big Pendleton shirt was scratchy warm and dark.

Now, stretched out here, with a nothing-to-do-for-a-while smile it is obvious that it is wrong to think of these sports as games. These sportsmen I have met have, in some measure, defined themselves by their sport. It is a trade as truly as a bricklayer's bricklaying or a writer's written words. It is different in that it does not remain, even for a little while, except in the yellowish pages of some record books and the participant's mind. They are soldiers in some war that will change no boundary lines outside of themselves. As it puts something missing in their lives. It is, at the same time, synthetic and real, reactionary and progressive, limiting and limitless. It is what they make it and they are what it makes them.

Soon sport is going to change. In the long, pre-industrial epoch, it was usually a contest of strength or stamina. Then the energy was transferred to great mechanical engines and the men became a part of the racing machine—an important part. Now a new epoch, a cybernetic, electronic-circuit, global-village sort of epoch. It is too new to have its name standardized yet. So far data-fat computers have programmed results of never-tried contests between noncontemporary individual or team contestants. But that is idle diversion. Now computers are being readied to analyze plays and offer strategy, or counter-strategy, and that could just do to American football what the auto engine did to footracing. There is a lot, yet to be seen.

But now it doesn't matter. What does is that these men have played their games, and what will matter is what they take from them and keep with themselves always.

And that is what this was all about.

You only go around once in life. So grab all the gusto you can.—Schlitz beer advertisement
    c. 1970

Here's Death, twitching my ear: "Live," says he, "for I'm coming."—Virgil
    c. 45 B.C.

EPILOGUE

All of it is there. The dust lifting up out of the arena in the spring, the horses' hooves hitting hard, the sun burning the skin after a cold winter . . . wheels splashing, churning, crashing through mud and water spraying the thick black ooze back onto you, the ground soft and sucking as you try to run over it . . . the airstrip hot with heavy summer sun . . . or summer again, but drizzling and gray as the angry little engines begin to sound like swarms of mad insects about to bite into and devour the track . . . sand spraying and dust thick and choking as you get closer with all about you —even the people—dry and hot and cracking like old leather boots too long left outside . . . in an airplane and watching the light line tight face muscles . . . and more. And there are the smells, too, smells that haunt the head with different memories of the same event: castor oil, carbon, dust, horse manure, hot air, sweat, grease on hands, mustard, gasoline, and mud at the corner of your mouth.

All of these things stick in the edges of the mind and come back occasionally to remind, renew and haunt you as you hunt back through your yesterdays.